To Emily

Hope you find the time
to read it!

# Beating the 24/7

# Beating the 24/7

## How Business Leaders Achieve a Successful Work/Life Balance

**Winston Fletcher**

JOHN WILEY & SONS, LTD

Published in 2002 John Wiley & Sons Ltd, The Atrium, Southern Gate, Chichester,
West Sussex PO19 8SQ, England

Telephone (+44) 1243 779777

Email (for orders and customer service enquiries): cs-books@wiley.co.uk
Visit our Home Page on www.wileyeurope.com or www.wiley.com

This publication is designed to provide accurate and authoritative information in regard to
the subject matter covered. It is sold on the understanding that the Publisher is not
engaged in rendering professional services. If professional advice or other expert
assistance is required, the services of a competent professional should be sought.

### Other Wiley Editorial Offices

John Wiley & Sons Inc., 111 River Street, Hoboken, NJ 07030, USA

Jossey-Bass, 989 Market Street, San Francisco, CA 94103-1741, USA

Wiley-VCH Verlag GmbH, Boschstr. 12, D-69469 Weinheim, Germany

John Wiley & Sons Australia Ltd, 33 Park Road, Milton, Queensland 4064, Australia

John Wiley & Sons (Asia) Pte Ltd, 2 Clementi Loop #02-01, Jin Xing Distripark,
Singapore 129809

John Wiley & Sons Canada Ltd, 22 Worcester Road, Etobicoke, Ontario, Canada M9W 1L1


### British Library Cataloguing in Publication Data

A catalogue record for this book is available from the British Library

ISBN 0-470-84762-X

Typeset in 11/16.5 ITC Garamond by Footnote Graphics, Warminster, Wiltshire.
Printed and bound in Great Britain by Biddles Ltd, Guildford and King's Lynn.
This book is printed on acid-free paper responsibly manufactured from sustainable
forestry in which at least two trees are planted for each one used for paper production.

# Contents

# Acknowledgements

I am immeasurably grateful to the 16 business leaders who agreed to be interviewed. For me – I cannot speak for them – the interviews were fascinating, stimulating and frequently fun. I sincerely hope they enjoyed the process as much as I did.

Without the 16 interviewees, it is obvious, there would have been no book. What is less obvious is that without Janette Jensen there would have been no book – or to be more precise, I would still be struggling with it to this day. She transcribed the interview tapes with such speed and accuracy that putting it all together was a doddle. It is not much of an exaggeration to say that I did the interviews, and Janette and the interviewees made the book.

# WORK/LIFE BALANCE: PIVOTAL PRINCIPLES

## *Phascogales and Parrots*

During the winter season bushtailed phascogale males fight each other ferociously for access to the females in order to breed. Soon afterwards they die of stress. The female brings up her seven or eight young on her own. She keeps them in her pouch for several months, then leaves them in their den each night while she forages alone in the forest for food to feed them.

The Taronga Foundation Zoo, Sydney, NSW

Like the Australian bushtailed phascogales, males and females of every species develop life systems which – however unfair and inequitable they may look – seem somehow to work for them. Male and female human beings have, similarly, developed life systems which – however unfair and inequitable they have looked – somehow seem to have worked for them. Until now. Changes that occurred during the twentieth century have dislocated family lives in affluent Western societies more than ever before.

Certain careers, usually male careers, have long been associated with disrupted family lives. Politics, the armed forces, the merchant navy, the police, the performance arts and entertainments, the medical profession – including nurses – and to a lesser extent even journalism and the diplomatic service have always demanded a commitment to irregular working hours and long separations between family members. Presumably the individuals who joined those professions and industries recognised, from the outset, the time commitment the jobs would entail. Presumably their spouses likewise recognised, from the outset, the time commitment their partners' jobs would entail – though that is not to say they were wildly happy about it. In any event, most of those jobs employed particular groups of dedicated people willing to suffer the privations the jobs demanded. The great majority of ordinary people were able, despite long hours and demanding bosses, to enjoy reasonably well-balanced work and family lives.

During the industrial revolution families often worked together in factories. Craftsmen and shopkeepers often ran family businesses, to be inherited by their children. In villages and on farms men worked exhausting hours, but never ventured far from their homes. They spent time with their wives and children most evenings, at weekends and during their meagre holidays. This is no longer the case, particularly for managers and executives in organisations of all kinds – large and small, public and private. Today work encroaches on every manager's personal life. The hours of work quoted in managers' employment contracts are like the prattle of parrots: they use words, but nobody thinks they mean anything.

## *The Triple-Whammy*

During the twentieth century, three major areas of change brought about a seismic transformation in the interface between men, women and children in families. Faster and easier travel, innovations in personal communications and female emancipation have between them constituted a triple-whammy which has fundamentally affected family relationships. Many of the consequences of this triple-whammy only began to be perceived, and addressed, at the very end of the last century. The longer-term effects on society of these family-disruptive forces have not yet begun to be precisely and properly assessed.

For families, the massive burgeoning of travel has had a host of often unpredictable results. Until the end of the nineteenth century almost everyone lived close to their work, and only a handful of individuals travelled on business abroad. Today vast numbers of people work in one place and live in another: they commute, either daily or weekly. Today international transportation has resulted in an explosion in global trade as a result of which – despite the blip following 11 September 2001 – innumerable globetrotters incessantly zip back and forth to business meetings in faraway places. They go to sell and to buy, to meet colleagues and to attend conferences, to run subsidiaries and to report to bosses. Planeloads of business people now spend a prodigious amount of time away from their homes, their partners and their children. This has happened willy-nilly. Nobody expected it. Nobody planned for it. It had never happened before, and our societies have not accommodated themselves to it. The individuals concerned have coped with the consequences as best they can, but there has been no guidance – not even much discussion or consideration of the personal difficulties involved. Cars, trains and planes have separated breadwinners from their families. Their crusts have got richer, their family lives poorer.

The explosions in commuting and in international travel have perhaps contributed far more than has previously been recognised to the break-up of the conventional family unit, and to the upsurge both of divorce and of single-parent families. If partners are to be constantly separated, often for long periods, why should they bother to enter into, or remain in, long-term binding relationships? Ceaseless travel opens a chasm across which the partners call to each other through distorting megaphones. It has led feminists to argue that work and marriage are, in the twenty-first century, impossible bedfellows – not least because the former so frequently removes one partner from the conjugal bed. Unquestionably, as the subsequent interviews reveal, travel puts a hefty strain on business people's relationships with both their partners and their children – a strain which can be handled, but a strain nonetheless. Globe-trotting is a marital time bomb, forever on the brink of exploding.

Developments in travel have had two other, perhaps less obvious, consequences for corporate managers. Many of them have acquired second homes, weekend homes, some distance from their places of employment; and most of them holiday abroad, sometimes on the European continent but often further afield. These two developments have, at first sight, counteracted those above. They have distanced the individuals from their places of work, and brought them into closer proximity with their families at specific times. But work has fought back. Weekends and holidays are constantly interrupted, bringing further strains on family relation-ships. Time that was intended to be shared with their families – 'quality time' as it is sometimes embarrassingly called – is fractured and shattered.

Simultaneously the innovations in personal communications have been both a blessing and a curse. Just as television failed to kill off the movies, new ways of sending messages simply add to the torrent of information with which every manager must cope – arriving at different times and in different ways. Letter post and the static telephone have been supplemented by e-mails, mobile phones, faxes, telephone conferencing, video conferencing and the entire gamut of new media. Each innovation extends the possibilities for continual, unremitting communication exponentially. On the one hand they make it possible for individuals to keep in touch with each other more easily than ever before; on the other they mean that people are at the beck and call of their work literally 24 hours a day, 7 days a week – especially if they work in multinational corporations. Global time never takes a coffee break. If you work in an international company there will always be people who want to talk to you while you are asleep. If you work in a UK company there will always be people who want to talk to you the moment you awake – particularly if you work in retailing.

The third major change, which I have called the emancipation of women, has – while entirely and unarguably desirable – again been multifaceted. The consequences are almost too numerous to count. Ever since the 1914–18 War more and more women have gone out to work, and have increasingly relished doing so. This makes it a lot harder – not impossible, but a lot harder – for them to fulfil their traditional role as mothers, a role they neglect only with very great feelings of personal guilt. Very nearly 50% of high-achieving women leave it too late to have children, and then profoundly regret it. Other women come to the conclusion, however reluctantly, that motherhood and scrabbling to the top of the business tree are incompatible. Those who are determined to do both often perceive male prejudices (including the prejudices of their husbands) as restraining and repressive. Women who constantly thump their heads against the glass ceiling suffer bitter migraines.

Meanwhile those women who completely give up their careers to be full-time wives and mothers increasingly resent being made to feel inadequate, old-fashioned, even indolent. They grow envious of the apparently stimulating and exciting business lives that their employed friends and their husbands lead. Their employed friends are always too busy to see them, while their husbands' working lives aggravate the festering sore by intruding on their evenings, their weekends and their holidays. They soon grow to suspect that their husbands view their families as irritating impediments to their business careers – that like unloved pets they get thrown the stale scraps of time left over when their husbands' work needs have been fully catered for.

So if women dedicate themselves to work, they fear their families will lose out. If they dedicate themselves to their families, they fear they themselves will lose out. Those, at least, seem to be women's unenviable options – and either way, work circumscribes their lives.

At work the obstacle race which women are compelled to run is, it is universally agreed, far tougher than the one run by men. But many of the obstacles are common to both sexes. Male and female managers alike find it problematic to spend enough time with their children, with their partners, and doing all the other things they like to do. Both sexes sometimes find themselves in situations when a sudden family crisis interrupts a crucial business event, or a sudden business crisis interrupts a crucial family event. For both sexes, work is simultaneously obsessive and exhausting. Anyone who becomes addicted, which means almost everyone in senior management or on the way up, finds work as heady and as demanding as any drug. Drug addicts make lousy partners, lousy parents, and even lousy friends.

## *The Managers' Millstone*

As the problems have proliferated and deepened, and as traditional family units have come under mounting strain, managers and executives have understandably grown anxious and stressed, often without recognising the causes. By the 1970s politicians and social commentators, particularly in the United States, were becoming aware that family and work were squaring up to each other like two jungle cats brawling over the same carrion. The Harvard management guru Rosabeth Moss Kanter is widely credited with having been the first to crystallise and identify the gravity of the issue in 1977 when she wrote, in her seminal book *Work and Family in the United States*:

> Organisations of the future will have to pay attention to their effects on people other than employed persons (spouses, children) and allow the needs of families to influence organisational decisions and shape organisational policies.

In subsequent years, the validity of this point has increasingly been accepted by society, by governments and by corporations. A fair number of work/life consultancies and study groups have been set up in the USA, the UK and elsewhere. The European Community and national governments in most Western countries have enacted basic legislation to force organisations to recognise some of the needs of families – though the UK negotiated an opt-out clause to the EC's 1998 Directive, which introduced a 48-hour maximum working week. This has meant that the implementation of the Directive in the UK has been patchy at best. Working hours in the UK are longer than in any other country in Europe: approximately four hours longer than the EC weekly average – and productivity is some 25% lower. While our long working hours cannot be the sole cause of the UK's low productivity, that they exacerbate the problem is beyond question.

Nonetheless many UK corporations have introduced policies that both comply with current legislation and, in some cases, run ahead of it. In 1999 about 20 of Britain's leading organisations – including the BBC, BT, Northern Foods, the Prudential, Sainsbury's, Shell and Unilever – joined together in an alliance called 'Employers for Work/Life Balance'. Interestingly, the alliance describes itself as 'pioneering', reflecting how recently work/life business issues have come to the forefront of organisations' attention. 'Employers for Work/Life Balance' published a set of principles and practices to which all the member organisations publicly committed themselves. Such policies were at first called 'family-friendly' policies, particularly in the United States, but that nomenclature has now largely been dropped. It came to be associated simply with policies designed to help young mothers – maternity leave, job-sharing, crèches and the like, and it is now accepted that the issues go far wider and far deeper. For this reason the term 'family-friendly' has generally been superseded by the term 'work/life balance'.

Work/life balance issues affect men as well as women, the old as well as the young, those without families as well as those with families. They affect people's relationships with their parents, as well as with their partners and children. And – though little or no attention has been paid to this aspect of the matter in the past – work/life balance problems intrude on all facets of people's individual and personal behaviour. Their work and their family may be the two most important things in their lives, but they are not the entirety. Life is more than a job, a partner and kids. Like everyone else, managers and executives have a diverse range of personal interests and passions, which their work frequently stifles. Other work/life balance issues can include leisure, hobbies, religion, business ethics – and finally clinical stress. Studies consistently prove the incidence of work-related stress to be growing apace. In the year 2000, British trades unions were involved in 6428 legal cases relating to work-induced stress, a massive 12-fold increase on the number the year before.

The present magnitude of work/life balance issues can hardly be overestimated. At the start of the new millennium, the British government launched a 'Work/Life Balance Campaign'. As a first step in this campaign the Department for Education and Employment carried out a baseline study into work/life balance practices in Britain in the year 2000. As part of the study 7500 working people were interviewed, together with 2500 employers with 5 or more employees. The report covered, as it was intended to, the entire British workforce, and among this wide group it is clear that better work/life balance issues are now of material significance. Although the questions used may be thought to have been a trifle anodyne, a massive 81% of employees agreed that 'Everyone should be able to balance their work and home lives'; and an even more massive 96% agreed that 'People work best when they can balance their work with other aspects of their lives'. Perhaps surprisingly, and certainly encouragingly, the employers' responses were not that dissimilar to those of the employees: 62% of the employers agreed with the first statement, and again an overwhelming 91% agreed with the second.

However the DfEE findings, together with those of several other studies, reveal that work/life balance and long working hours are especially, indeed overwhelmingly, a problem for the managerial classes. Work/life balance is the managerial crown of thorns – the managers' millstone, the burden they must bear to grind their golden corn. The DfEE study showed that in 75% of workplaces senior managers and professionals worked additional hours, over and above the standard working week – compared to around 30% for the rest of the working population. A TUC survey in December 2001 broadly confirmed this figure. It showed that 71% of employees in the AB social class 'normally work extra hours'. A European labour force survey in 2001 showed that nearly 60% of those who worked longer than 48 hours a week in the UK – 2.2 million full-time employees – were managers and professional people. These groups constitute only some 20% of the population. The managers who work over 48 hours a week are predominantly, though not exclusively, males in the private (rather than public) sector. These millstone managers do not put in the extra hours to earn extra money – at least not in the short run. While 98% of manual workers get paid overtime for working longer hours, among the AB social classes only 16% get paid overtime.

In February 2001 the Institute of Management published a study – the fourth and last in an annual series – carried out on its behalf by the University of Manchester Institute of Science and Technology. This is probably the most thorough study of how work/life balance issues are affecting British managers today. The Institute of Management's database was used, and generated 1516 individual responses, which again confirmed many of the findings of all the other data available. Sometimes different surveys throw up different findings, which can be hard to reconcile. That is not the case with work/life balance surveys. The dissonances between them are minimal, the results – almost astonishingly – consistent.

The Institute of Management 2001 study showed that 82% of managers work, on average, an hour or more above their contractual hours each working day (not far off the DfEE's comparable figure of 75% and the TUC's comparable figure of 71% – given that the samples were all drawn differently, and the questions differed slightly). And 40% of the Institute's respondents work more than 51 hours a week – again roughly comparable with the other survey findings.

This strong managerial class bias has hardly been recognised by either governments or commentators. Not surprisingly, the millstone is heaviest for those managers who work truly excessive hours. The DfEE baseline study defined 'long or excessive working hours' as 60 hours or more each week – a 12-hour working day, excluding weekends. Some 15% of managers and professionals work these excessive hours, while for manual workers the percentage is insignificant. Over four years the Institute of Management surveys showed an average of just over 10% of managers working more than 60 hours a week. And the DfEE showed that while 20% of employees sometimes work from home, nearly 80% of them are managers or professionals – in other words, managers and professionals find themselves working at home far more than most people.

Moving on, in a survey carried out in 2001 by Ceridian Performance Partners for the leading UK business magazine *Management Today*, 26% of business executives claimed that 'putting work before their home and family life' was the biggest single sacrifice they had made in their career. A further 11% said 'absence from home' was the single biggest sacrifice, and another 9% answered 'missing out on children growing up' to the same question. Other responses included: 'divorce/strain on relationship (5%)', 'missed leisure time (4%)', and 'not having/postponing children (3%)'. In aggregate not far short of two-thirds of the respondents felt that the difficulties in their personal lives that resulted from work had been the biggest sacrifices their career had demanded. Of those who expressed a view, more than half felt their work/life balance was wrong. In most cases, when compared with a similar survey in 1998, those figures had increased. In the Institute of Management study, 72% of the managers said their long working hours adversely affected their relationships with their partners, and 77% believed they adversely affected their relations with their children. A 1997 European Commission study among young adults in the UK, Norway, Sweden, Ireland and Portugal revealed similar concerns.

## *The Work/Life Ratio*

Improving people's work/life balance can be approached from three standpoints – which are far from mutually exclusive. The first two depend upon the employer organisation – its practices and its philosophy. The third depends on the individual. (The Families and Work Institute in New York has developed a similar model, based on four progressive stages.)

First, organisations can – whether or not impelled by legislation – introduce specific practices, such as parental leave, part-time working or flexitime working, which make the achievement of a good work/life balance easier. Several pieces of legislation have already helped here, and more are in the pipeline. Second only to parental leave, flexible working hours are widely thought to be the most significant single way to help most people balance their personal and work commitments, and flexitime working is becoming more common, albeit very slowly. Flexitime working systems have been around for well over 30 years. Rosabeth Moss Kanter several times mentions their growing popularity in her 1977 book – but the DfEE baseline study showed that in the year 2000 only 24% of all employees in Britain worked under flexible time arrangements.

In any event, legislative improvements and flexitime are far more relevant to the generality of employees than to managers and executives in more senior positions. For millstone managers the overriding work/life burden is their weighty workload. The majority of the AB's questioned in the TUC survey said they worked extra hours because they 'had so much work to do', and 75% of the Institute of Management respondents said they worked long hours because it was 'the only way to deal with the workload'. But some 70% of those managers who expressed a view in the 2001 Ceridian survey stated that 'Flexible working does not solve the problem of workload', while among the Institute of Management respondents the same opinion was even more pronounced: a mere 5% of respondents thought flexible working hours would be the best way to improve their work/life balance. For the great majority of managers, the idea of hoping to cure work/life balance problems with flexitime is about as realistic as hoping to cure cancer with aspirin.

Second, organisations can help employees to balance their lives by making it a matter of corporate philosophy. This means changes in attitudes and commitment throughout the organisation, as well as the introduction of specific rules and practices. This is the route unhesitatingly advocated by the 'Employers for Work/Life Balance' alliance. The leadership of the organisation – the chairman, CEO and board – must make it unequivocally clear they expect every employee, particularly every senior employee, to be sympathetic to work/life problems. They must state that as a matter of corporate policy they expect top managers to allow people time off for important family events, without argument or even much questioning. Simultaneously they will expect staff to be open and responsible about their need for such absences, and they will expect them to make up for any time taken, as a matter of course and without pressure. I believe organisations could, for example, introduce a straightforward 'family-time' system whereby employees give notice of family-time needs, and indicate when and how they intend to repay the time taken. Such broadminded corporate attitudes are likely to be far more beneficial to most managers than the introduction of arbitrary rules.

Studies have consistently shown that the improved employer/employee relations that result from family-sympathetic policies make an organisation a much more attractive place to work. They reduce staff turnover and increase employee commitment. Put simply, enacting a generous work/life balance philosophy will pay dividends: for the organisation it is enlightened self-interest.

(It should be noted, however, that although the studies have revealed that work/life balance improvements bring definite advantages to organisations, none has yet succeeded in accurately quantifying any economic or fiscal benefits. Estimates of the fiscal benefits have been made, but none of them stand up to much scrutiny. In subsequent chapters several of the business leaders interviewed comment on this point. Nonetheless and beyond question, every manager who is remotely interested in achieving a satisfactory work/life balance should – must – seek to be employed by organisations that are sympathetic rather than inimical to the issues.)

Third, and this is fundamentally what *Beating the 24/7* is about, millstone managers can learn to handle their own work/life balances more effectively. In this fiercely competitive age, anyone eager to build a successful career will find the weight of work overwhelming. Companies can, and should, do their bit to lessen the burden. But however much or little a company does to help, in the end the onus is on the individual. Your kid's ball is in your court. Time is a finite resource, so there will always be trade-offs. The manager will be forced to make choices all along the way. But all managers know they could organise the balance between their working and personal lives better, at least to some degree.

Consciously and deliberately or – as is more likely – instinctively and without much forethought, you currently make incessant decisions that apportion your time between your work on the one hand, and your family and your leisure on the other. This division I have defined as your Work/Life Ratio. It probably cannot be calculated precisely; it will doubtless vary a little over the course of each year, and as the following chapters show there will occasionally be times when work, family and leisure overlap. For managers, work and family life are not the totally separate, watertight compartments that many commentators believe. Time spent travelling to and from work can complicate the division too, as some people work in transit and some do not. But calculating your Work/Life Ratio is a useful litmus test, and the principal is straightforward. There are 24/7 hours in a week: 168 in total. Excluding an average 48 hours or so sleeping hours leaves you 120 waking hours. Let's call 120 hours the Basic Waking Week. If you tot up the hours you spend working, say 65 or so, and subtract them from the 120 available, your Work/Life Ratio will be 65/55 hours – or 54%/46%. If you can cut your working week to 60 hours – which the DfEE defined as excessive! – you will improve your Ratio to a creditable 50%/50%. If your present Work/Life Ratio is far from 50%/50% – with the work percentage too high – make the 50%/50% equilibrium a target. It should not be impossible to achieve. You will still be working much longer hours than you really should.

Think of the Work/Life Ratio as a see-saw. If you are not spending sufficient time on work, you will be stuck permanently and uncomfortably at the bottom of the swing. If, in an endeavour to reach the sky, your work percentage soars, you will permanently be high in the air, dangerously unbalanced – with your feet never touching the ground. If you are oscillating around the 50%/50% equilibrium level you will always be able to push yourself up for a while, or down for a while, as the demands of your work and family demands dictate.

## *To Find the Right Answers, Ask the Right People*

The apportionment of time – achieving a balanced Work/Life Ratio – is, naturally, vitally important. But a good work/life balance is not solely a matter of time. As we shall see, there are numerous other factors involved. The question for every manager – man or woman – is fundamental: how can I be truly successful both at work and at home? How can I accept more responsibility, take on more challenges, increase my authority, increase my remuneration – and still enjoy a really good family life? How can I climb the management ladders without sliding down the personal snakes?

It is hellishly difficult. But it can be done. And it is far and away the most important do-it-yourself job that you will undertake in your life. If you screw it up your partner will suffer, your children will suffer, you will suffer – and the terrible irony is that as sure as hell your work, for which you have sacrificed everything else, will suffer too.

To find some of the answers to these important and intractable problems I interviewed 16 of Britain's most senior business people and asked them about their own work/life balances. This is the first time that such a study has been undertaken, and I believe it provides a compelling and graphic picture of work/life balance issues in Britain at the start of the twenty-first century. It should be made clear immediately that it was not, nor was it ever intended to be, an academic, scientific study of the subject. It is an exploration of success. Had it been a scientific study I would also have needed to interview business managers whose personal lives have been destroyed by their work addiction. I would have needed to interview business leaders who have chosen not to have children, or maybe not even to have a spouse or permanent partner. I would have needed to interview some of the growing number of one-parent family business people, who already number 7% of the workforce according to the DfEE baseline study. There are countless top business managers who do not have what most people would call a satisfactory work/life balance – and maybe somebody else will one day carry out an intriguing study into the ways they live their lives. That was not my bag. This book is expressly intended to help business managers who have partners and children to achieve better work/life balances, and to do so by revealing how individuals at the very pinnacle of business success have succeeded in the endeavour.

My gratitude to my 16 respondents is unstinting. They freely gave up precious time to be interviewed and then went through their transcripts in detail. Much more importantly they answered the questions I asked with immense frankness and honesty. They did so – each and every one of them – because they recognise the immense and growing importance of work/life balance issues in the modern world.

The interviews that follow have hardly been edited – they are in the colloquial, conversational style of each of the interviewees, which helps provide a flavour of each individual's personality and approach. As you will see, some of the questions probed quite deeply, perhaps embarrassingly, into the work/life difficulties they faced – but they did not baulk at giving their answers.

Though the selected business leaders were not, as I have said, in any way intended to represent a statistically reliable sample, they cover an immensely broad spectrum of business experience and activity. Four of the respondents – Helen Alexander, Sarah Hogg, Nicola Horlick and Rosalyn Wilton – are women; a much higher proportion of women than is yet to be found, regrettably, in top management positions in Britain. Four of the respondents – George Bull, Dominic Cadbury, Michael Perry and Richard Sykes – have retired from the jobs in which they built their careers, but are still heavily occupied in businesses and organisational issues. Several of the respondents – including Michael Grade, Sarah Hogg, Colin Marshall, Michael Perry and Dennis Stevenson – hold non-executive chairmanships and directorships in a wide range of companies.

Several of the respondents – particularly but not only George Bull, Colin Marshall, Richard Sykes and Rosalyn Wilton – had to do an immense amount of international travelling early in their careers, when their children were still young. John Clare and Peter Davis run major retailers; Helen Alexander and Clive Hollick run media companies; Nicola Horlick and Rosalyn Wilton run city-based operations; Christopher Bland now heads a leading technology company, though he has a wealth of experience in media and in the NHS; Richard Branson is probably Britain's most successful entrepreneur; and Richard Sykes ran Britain's leading scientific research company. At Unilever, Michael Perry spent many years living and working as an expatriate, which poses its own particular problems. Cadbury's, where Dominic Cadbury spent most of his working life, was one of the first companies in Britain, perhaps in the world, to embrace work/life balance issues, well over a century ago – though of course they were not called that then. Peter Davis has been closely and personally involved in many of the government's initiatives in this area. Nicola Horlick's experience – having had six children, one of whom died tragically, while simultaneously building her career – is unparalleled.

Finally, because I was deliberately looking for individuals who have achieved a successful work/life balance, 14 of the interviewees have been married only once, and are still with their first partner – far from a statistical reflection of society at large. (Though a small study in the United States has suggested that – contrary perhaps to most expectations – business leaders are marginally more likely than the population at large to stay with their first spouse.) Among my 16 interviewees, only Richard Branson and Michael Grade have ever been divorced. Their thoughts about the impact of their work on their first marriages are especially revealing, and have been instrumental in helping them reach a successful work/life balance today.

As soon as you begin to read the interviews it will be clear that none of the business leaders have found achieving a successful work/life balance a cinch. They made sacrifices they have sometimes later regretted. They have found themselves in tough situations when they have had to decide instantly how to deal with a family crisis that occurred at exactly the same time as a critical business engagement. They know they have occasionally made the wrong choices and decisions. But they have come through. And in doing so they have developed personal systems, techniques and routines that have helped them.

## *What the Interviews Reveal*

The most consistent theme to emerge from all the interviews, without exception, is the vital role of the partner in making a successful work/life balance possible. Even allowing for the fact that spouses in happy marriages like to butter each other up a little in public, and to praise their partners in print, the consistency with which the influence of partners is mentioned cannot be discredited.

The partner's role is subtly different for men and for women. In all cases the partner has to offer psychological support, to sympathise with their spouse's ambitions and their 100% commitment to their work. But the men say their wives frequently – or anyway sometimes – admonish them when they push things too far. This requires great sensitivity. The wives show enthusiasm for their husband's work, and they do not throw tantrums or quarrel about its intrusions. But they firmly bring their men into line when they believe they need to. The men do not merely accept this level of discipline. They welcome it. They are grateful. They admit that they do not always say as much to their wives, but they recognise that their wives' pressures are of huge benefit to them. This would not happen if the wives were too insistent, or nagged perpetually. From time to time they exert a resolute touch on the tiller – and it works.

But the fundamental lesson here is that the men listened, and responded, to their wives' criticisms. Many husbands foolishly shrug off their wives' protests, ignore them, believe them to be short-sighted or even selfish. They feel their wives have no understanding of the hothouses in which they are trying to flower. That may be understandable, but it is crazy. Michael Grade's comments, on pages 64 and 65 show the inevitable outcome of disregarding your partner's legitimate concerns. It is no way to enhance your work/life balance.

The same does not appear to be true for the female business leaders. They too need strong psychological support from their partners, but they look to their husbands to encourage them constantly and support their commitment when they waver. And the women often need practical as well as psychological support. They expect their husbands to step in and help with the children when necessary, or even to share responsibility for the children equally. Above all it is essential that their husbands never carp about their work, and the demands it makes on their time – quite the opposite of the wives' role. In their interviews Helen Alexander, Sarah Hogg, Nicola Horlick and Rosalyn Wilton all testify that they could never have succeeded in business without the active, positive and potent support of their husbands. They feel they could not possibly be happy at work if there were turmoil at home. The lesson for women intending to build a business career – easier said than done perhaps – is to ensure that their chosen partner will never be uncomfortable about their work and success. In work, as in life, jealous husbands are an unmitigated handicap.

Beyond these crucial psychological – and for women occasionally practical – supports, the role of partners varies from situation to situation. Almost nobody discusses their everyday business problems with their partners to any great extent. Equally, almost everybody discusses really knotty and important issues when they arise. Some people like to get their partners involved socially in their business lives, some do not. But almost all have developed small stratagems and wiles for ameliorating the never-ending family strains that a jam-packed business life causes, and these are revealed in each interview.

Another consistent theme to emerge from the interviews is the impossibility of keeping holidays and weekends sacrosanct. Some of the interviewees – Christopher Bland, Richard Branson and Nicola Horlick particularly – try hard to make their weekends and holidays work-free zones. But to a greater or lesser degree every one of the interviewees has had their holidays broken into. At the minimum, holidays are punctuated by urgent telephone calls. Most of them have frequently started their holidays late, cut them short early or flown back to work in the middle. This, again, reflects a great deal of understanding from their partners. They almost certainly do not like it, but they cope with it. It must be assumed that partners who cannot live with broken holidays cannot live with successful business people. Weekends, likewise, are constantly interrupted. And in the case of weekends, this is often deliberate; many business leaders prefer to work through papers during the relative peace and quiet of the weekend, or check things out on Sunday evenings, rather than be inundated with problems as soon as they arrive back on Monday mornings. One of the prices of business success in the modern world is that you have to be constantly on call – and that is not something legislation or anything else will ever alter. If people at the very top of business life cannot protect their weekends and holidays, nobody can. If you are going to succeed you will have to go with the flow. The Institute of Management study showed that 73% of managers are sometimes contacted by their employers outside of working hours, and among board directors the percentage rises to a mighty 85%. The lesson here is to accept that interruptions will occur, and aim to manage and minimise them. To resent, resist and rail against them will inevitably lead to irritation and stress.

None of the respondents, however, finds the new modes of

communication – e-mails, mobiles, faxes and the rest – much of an intrusion in their private lives. Admittedly they are at the top, which must make a difference. But they all insist that communications technology can be mastered – mobiles can be switched off, computers can remain unvisited – until you are ready. Far from being fazed by the new technologies, they universally see them as helpful in their work/life balances. Nearly all of them have separate business and personal e-mail addresses, and often separate business and personal mobile phones. They do not divulge their personal e-mail addresses and mobile numbers to anyone but family, close friends and – usually – their PAs. All of which protects them from unwanted interruptions. It also allows them to use their personal e-mails and mobiles to communicate easily with their partners and families. Indeed they emphasise, with some telling anecdotes, how useful e-mails are in keeping them in touch with their wandering children. Lesson: manage the new technology, and use it for personal communications with your family.

The next key theme to emerge from the interviews is the importance of delegation. It is widely accepted that all career progress depends, in large measure, upon the ability to delegate skilfully. It is now clear that the achievement of a good work/life balance is also dependent upon delegation. The essence of delegation is trust. The interviewees trust their subordinates and colleagues at work to take decisions and get on with things when they are not present – and trust them to know when it is essential to intrude on their weekends and holidays. They trust their PAs to filter messages and decisions, and only to interrupt them at truly crucial moments. Without delegation, and trust, it is impossible to be away from your desk on family matters when you need to be, and impossible to relax when you are. The lesson: at every level in organisations, achieving a good work/life balance will depend upon having good people around you, and having confidence in them.

This is especially vital – another theme to emerge – at moments of real crisis. In every manager's life there will be occasions when they are at work and a family disaster occurs. Such calamities – as George Bull, John Clare, Richard Sykes and Rosalyn Wilton vividly show – take no regard of your work; they can and do occur when you are involved in work of the greatest importance, work that simply cannot be postponed. Those are very tough calls. They are times when you rely doubly on the support of your colleagues and subordinates. But it is clear that at times of real crisis workmates will always close ranks and help out. The lesson is that when a real family crisis occurs you should not hesitate to report it to your colleagues at work and then respond as fast as you damn well humanly can. Do not hide the event (as one of Helen Alexander's colleagues did). Nowadays all organisations accept that personal crises happen, and that when they do happen responsible employees want to respond to them instantly.

Most of the interviewees also demonstrate that work and family life are not the only time pressures that need to be balanced. They aim to find time for their friends – though few of them succeed as much as they would like. They try to keep up their hobbies. They kill two birds with a single stone by deliberately involving their children in their own leisure interests. They develop sporting and other relaxations that can be followed as part of their job. In other words, though they appear to be obsessed by their work they squeeze in as many other activities as they possibly can. This is undeniably more difficult for women than for men – but even the women find time for a few leisure activities, more and more as the years go by and their children flee the nest. The lesson: all work and no play makes Jack a neurotic boy. And the same goes for Jill.

A relatively new theme these interviews reveal is the importance of choosing a job that chimes with your personal values. The Institute of Management 2001 survey revealed that an overwhelming 75% of managers now state that 'I want to work for an organisation that reflects my individual values and beliefs'. It is far easier to accept, and to get your family to accept, the strains of working excessive hours and the relentless demands upon your personal time if you feel your work is, directly or indirectly, benefiting society. This helps break down the barriers and conflicts between work and family life. Work and family life cease to be antagonistic, and hardly demand to be balanced. To some extent your family life and your work become, as they have always been in many vocational professions, an integrated entity. This issue is manifestly of growing importance to younger people. Perhaps – though this is surely a pipe dream – the dissonance between work and life will one day disappear.

The final, and perhaps most obvious, conclusion to be derived from the interviews is that to achieve a successful work/life balance you will need to make the effort. It will not happen of its own accord. Legislative and organisational practices, policies and philosophies can help, but in the end the buck stops with you. You will need to put yourself out to attend parents' evenings, to see your children perform in school sports and entertainments, to be with your partner on important occasions, to be ready to handle crises. You will need to achieve an acceptable Work/Life Ratio. You will need constantly to put as much effort into your personal life as into your business life. Some of the interviewees admit that, particularly at the start of their careers, they tried to let their personal lives take care of themselves – and now, to some extent at least, they regret it. The lesson is that there is no easy way out; balancing your life and your work means more work. Nothing worth achieving is achieved without effort.

Here then, to kick off, is a briefcase full of pivotal principles – eleven for men, and eleven for women: positive actions that will help you balance your work and your life more harmoniously.

## Improving Your Work/Life Balance: The Pivotal Principles

- Work for organisations sympathetic to work/life issues.
- Calculate your Work/Life Ratio and aim for at least a 50%/50% equilibrium.
- If you are a man, do not ignore your wife's yellow card when your work is fouling up your family's life.
- If you are a woman, make sure your partner will whole-heartedly support your business ambitions, and not be envious of your success.
- Minimise holiday and weekend interruptions, but do not fight them; you won't win.
- Get a private e-mail address and mobile phone, and use them to keep in touch with your family.
- Delegation is as important to your personal life as it is to your business life: trust your colleagues.
- At times of real family crisis tell your boss and your workmates what is happening, then scram.
- Important though work and family are, make time for other leisure commitments – these become more important as you grow older.

- If you work in a job you feel to be worthwhile, work/life balance problems will wither and be less irksome.
- Develop stratagems and systems to ameliorate the unavoidable incursions of work into your personal life.
- Making the most of your non-working life is damned hard work.

As you read the 16 interviews that follow, in addition to these pivotal areas of broad agreement you will find lots of disagreement. This is only to be expected. In the first place all of those interviewed are strong-minded individuals, with independent attitudes and original views. Those are among the reasons they have been so successful. But perhaps even more importantly, because the entire subject of work/life balance is a relatively new one there are few, if any, universally accepted truths about its nature – fewer still about how to cope with the complications it causes. The interviewees all have different ways of dealing with the difficulties, and at the end of each interview I have extracted three or four tips which may help you with 'Keeping Your Balance' – systems and stratagems that I believe emerge from what the interviewee has said. You yourself may spot different tips, systems and stratagems. The tips I have extracted from one interview may occasionally contradict those from another interview – in which case you will need to assess the ones most likely to apply to you, personally. We are all on a steep and important learning curve. It is to be hoped that *Beating the 24/7* will contribute to this learning process.

Many of the interviewees, especially but not only Sarah Hogg, emphasise the importance of good luck in achieving a good work/life balance – and of course luck does play a role. Luck plays a role in all human activities. For my part, I believe her emphasis on luck is unduly modest. People make their luck. ('I am a great believer in luck', quipped the Canadian economist and wit Stephen Leacock, 'and I find the harder I work the more I have of it.') The death of Nicola Horlick's daughter was a dreadful stroke of bad luck – or fate as she might prefer to call it – but she coped with it. To some degree her work helped her cope. If your work/life balance is seriously out of kilter it is no use blaming it on bad luck, as though that means there is nothing you can do to alter it. If that is your view then reading this or any other book will be a waste of time. But if that is your view you are playing ostrich. Human beings can improve their lot, if they try. Good and bad luck simply make things a bit easier for some of us, a bit harder for others.

One of the most tangible differences between the interviewees, I believe, results from their relative ages. The younger respondents – generally those under about 50 – display a much higher conscious-ness of the role that organisations can play in promoting good work/life balance practices for their employees. Some of them are posi-tively evangelistic about it. That too is only to be expected. As we have seen, and as Christopher Bland among others emphasises, the phrase is a new one, and so is the recognition of its importance. However Dominic Cadbury, with the wealth of Cadbury's historic experience, emphasises what a minefield the involvement of an organisation in its employees' private lives can be. Having been, in the past, a rather paternalistic company with a close and kindly interest in its employees' wellbeing, Cadbury's has learned that many people do not want their employers to become too intimately involved in their lives. This thought is clearly echoed by Helen Alexander, Christopher Bland, Sarah Hogg and several of the other interviewees. It is not only individuals who find it tricky to get the work/life balance right. Exactly the same is true for the employer organisations them-selves.

The widespread interest in work/life balance is new, but it will not be a passing fad. It is not anti-work. It recognises that work can and should be stimulating, enjoyable and exciting as well as financially rewarding. Naturally the business leaders I interviewed all share that view. Ever since ancient Greece, human beings have known that there is a need to avoid excessive concentration on a single aspect of our humanity, to be rounded individuals, to develop all of our personal potentialities. 'Nothing in excess' was inscribed in the great temple at Delphi – the most prestigious oracular shrine in the Graeco-Roman world.

Some 2500 years later Noel Coward aphorised: 'Work is more fun than fun' – but he did not practise what he preached. That is not the way he lived his life. He worked hard and he played hard. The truth is that work is more fun if the rest of life is fun too.

# Chapter 1

# SIR RICHARD SYKES, FRS

Richard Sykes is Rector of Imperial College, London, and was formerly chief executive and subsequently chairman of GlaxoSmithKline. He is a director of Rio Tinto and of the British Pharmaceutical Group, vice-president of the National Society for Epilepsy and a trustee of the Natural History Museum. He has been president of the British Association for the Advancement of Science, a member of the Trade Policy Forum and of the Advisory Group on Competitiveness to the President of the Board of Trade. He is the author of over 100 scientific publications and is a visiting professor at King's College, London and at the University of Bristol.

Richard Sykes was born in 1942 and educated at Royds Hall Grammar School, Huddersfield, Paddington Technical College, Chelsea College and Queen Elizabeth College, London, acquiring postgraduate doctorates at the Universities of Bristol and of London. He is married and has two children.

**“**If we go back in time, people were more dedicated to their jobs and left the family and other lifestyle activities behind. But there has been a change. We are coming into a period now when young people are much more cognisant of the fact that 'Yes, the job is important, but so is the rest of my life, so is my family and so are all the other pieces in the jigsaw. I am prepared to work hard but I am not prepared to give everything up and divorce myself from the rest of life.' That is a very healthy attitude. I see it in my own children. They are both professionals and yet they both recognise the need for balance; whereas when I first started I was totally involved in the job and did not spend an enormous time with the children when they were young. The kids would be doing something at school, maybe, and I would not turn up. I would not be there. My wife would say, 'Don't worry, I'll take care of it. I'll deal with it.' I was very rarely at their birthday parties when the children were young because I thought it was more important to be at work.

I felt myself under pressure to be totally committed to work. That was certainly true in the United States. I worked for 10 years in the United States and in those days the work ethic there was different. It is probably not too different today, but then it was quite different. And I had to travel a huge amount. I went to Japan a lot, or I had to come back to Europe. I was often away from my family for a week, or two weeks or even more. In the UK people were having three- or four-week holidays. The Americans were having two-week holidays. Then they did not even take their two-week holidays because they felt they should be working. When I worked in the United States I never took my full two weeks either. Even when I came back to the UK I did not take my full entitle-ment. It is only in the last few years that I have done. In the period when I was brought up, you were expected to be working all the time, and if you wanted to progress you simply had to work all the time. You had no choice. That was the ethos.

The support of my wife was critically important. When I was working in this country in the mid-1970s, economic conditions were pretty awful. There were endless strikes, mortgage interest rates were around 18%, the weather was bloody awful. My wife and I discussed it and I said, 'Look, we really need to get out of here.' I went to the USA and had an interview and came back and told her I had a job. She said 'Let's go.' If she had said, 'I'm not moving from the UK' that would have created a lot of problems. But she was positive: 'We'll go. Let's give it a good try. Let's pick up the kids and let's go to America.' Then you go as a pair, you go as a family, and you are committed as a family. When it was time to come back she said: 'Fine, if that is what we have to do, we'll up roots.' Wives are the ones that suffer most from major moves like that. I go to work every day whether I am in the United States or in the UK or Australia, but my wife has had to set down new roots, get new friends, get a new circle and it is all quite difficult. It was a tough assignment. And though my wife is pretty forgiving, she would sometimes crack the whip and say 'For Christ's sake, you need to do this family thing . . . you need to go and see your mother', or whatever it might be. Without her support, progress in my career would have been impossible.

Indeed it would have been absolutely impossible, because you do not worry when you know everything is being looked after effectively at home. Somebody is in control, and the kids are in a perfect environment, they are happy. And they benefit a bit as well because they know that when I come back from Japan or wherever there will be gifts. So they are excited and look forward to you coming back from a trip because they know you will bring presents for them!

Nowadays I never interrupt a holiday to come back to work. But I make sure I stay in touch, on a daily basis. That way I can deal with any issues immediately they arise. It usually takes very little time – maybe an hour in the morning or an hour in the evening – to talk to my secretary, to deal with things. It is not a problem, it is not onerous – and then your mind is at rest, you have dealt with the issues, they are out the way. If there is something urgent, you deal with it. To me that is much better than coming back to bloody chaos.

It comes with experience. It takes time to learn. When you start your business life there is a big learning curve because you come out of an educational institution – or anyway I did – and you have to learn new ways of working. You develop new relationships, and you have to make a mark. So you work hard and you put a lot of effort into it. And in my field there was not just a lot of work, there was an enormous amount of reading, and usually that can be done only outside the work environment, because when you read you need silence and you need to concentrate. It also takes a lot of time. So you get used to trying to balance all these things, and as time goes on you become more professional at it.

You learn partly by just keeping your eyes and your ears open. You watch other people and you see the practices you want to follow. You see some people who are mad. They work 18 hours a day and they want to control everything – they are micro-managers – and you say to yourself, 'I do not want to be like that.' You see other people who are lazy and superficial, who flick over every-thing and do not commit themselves too much and again you say to yourself 'I do not want to be like that.' And you see people who are both dedicated to work and managing their lives well. You really learn about life by watching and listening to people.

It is the people you work with who matter. There will be some managers who encourage you to make sure that you do not put absolutely everything into work and that you do have a balanced lifestyle. There are other managers who are antagonistic. It is more to do with individuals than with organisations. Organisations do not 'feel things'. You would never find an organisation that said, 'You must be here 20 hours a day, otherwise you will not make progress in your career.' But there will always be slave drivers who make that implicit in the way they operate, the way they manage their people. On the other hand you will find individuals who are very sensitive to these issues. Fortunately, today you will find more of the latter. HR departments constantly put out the message: 'Do not work people too hard. Stress is an enormous problem. Make sure people have a sufficiently balanced lifestyle.'

And that applies to me now, too. Although I work a long day, you will not find me here at eight o'clock or nine o'clock at night. I start early – when I was in business full-time I was at work before seven every morning, and I left by six or seven o'clock at the latest. It was a 12-hour day. But I was never a role model for anybody who wants to work 18 hours a day because I think that is mad. In addition I take papers home, particularly over the weekend, to make sure I catch up with everything. But that is not onerous either.

You should not paint everything black and white and say, 'I only work at work and I only play at home.' When you are in a position of responsibility, when you are in an interesting job, you cannot do that. It does not matter whether you are in a research laboratory or in a small organisation or running a big company, you never stop thinking about things, you are always thinking about how you should deal with the situations occurring around you. You cannot switch your mind on and off. Sometimes at work you will think about your home life and you will deal with personal issues, and when you are at home you will read business papers. That is fine. But you must not let the work become too dominating. It is like exercise regimes. You cannot keep to an unchangeable regime because there will always be things that get in the way. But you can make sure that you fit your exercise regime in when you can, you fit it around all the other things that are happening. Constant flexibility is critically important.

I have never been one to get particularly stressed – you do obviously get somewhat stressed at times, when there are a lot of things that converge – but I coped with it and was not really aware of it as stress. I very rarely have a problem sleeping. And I have always liked to have some time to myself. Even as a student I used to like spending time by myself and I still do now. It is important to have some time to yourself so you can think, particularly when you are constantly being bombarded by things. But you can do that in a family lifestyle, even when you are doing something like cutting the grass. Cutting the grass is a pretty mindless exercise, but you can do a lot of thinking when you are mowing, or doing things like that, where you are in the family circle but you have time to think.

Most of my leisure activities have been family-orientated – such as going camping with the children, skiing with the children. We all swim, we all scuba dive. We did those sorts of activities together as a family when the children were younger and we still do today. Skiing is the best family activity of all because everybody is exhausted at the end of the day. All we want to do then is eat and sleep, whereas our beach holidays tend to be argumentative in the evenings, because we all still have lots of energy left!

When I was a young research scientist at Glaxo our son, who must then have been about 16 months old, poured a kettle of boiling hot water over himself. My wife sprayed him with cold water, which was absolutely the right thing to do, and then rushed him off to the emergency ward at hospital. Communication was not so easy in those days. I came home and found the house empty; then the neighbours told me what had happened so I rushed off to the hospital. My wife stayed in the hospital with him and I went back to work. But I stopped working full-time. I was visiting the hospital constantly. Somebody looked after my daughter so that was OK, and people pulled together. I had to try to carry on with my work and deal with the situation. My colleagues were very sympathetic. Work colleagues always are, about things like that. And you just have to cope. I do not remember a situation where I could not cope, because there were always infrastructures that allowed me to cope.

Today e-mails and mobile phones make it much easier to keep in touch with the children. I talk to them on the phone and I see them a lot, but sometimes we just send each other e-mails. They might be using the computer and think, 'Oh, I'll send a note to my Dad', and I reply and off it goes. E-mails, mobiles and faxes are not intrusive at all. A mobile phone only works if you turn it on. So I use my mobile, it doesn't use me. I use my fax, it doesn't use me. I am not dominated by technology. You look around and see people constantly on their mobile phones. It's nonsense. What are they doing it for? You use the mobile if somebody needs to contact you urgently. If you need to contact somebody urgently, you can. You do not have to communicate every five minutes. How the hell can it be intrusive? It is only intrusive if you allow it to be. People sometimes have urgent questions and they call me up, and I do the same. If it is urgent enough I will phone people on a Saturday night or a Sunday night. But that is only if it is really important. I have never been constantly on to people.

When I first selected my job, I worked in a lab and the science dominated my life. I became fascinated by bacteriology and infectious diseases. I was working in antibiotic research and particularly on resistance to antibiotics, and I started spending a lot of time with physicians. Then I became aware that what I was doing could do good for society. I did not start out with the aim of doing good, but I quickly realised medical research was something that was bound to do good.

If I could start again I would probably study medicine as opposed to pure science, and then study pure science later. I could then have been more helpful to society, as I would have known more medicine. Still, as a leader of a company that operates in healthcare I believe that a lot of what such companies do has dramatically improved the quality of life. That is very important for the people who work in the company. They want their research to end up helping people. I am convinced of that.

The outside world does not understand the process. You cannot do all the work and pump in all the money and expect investors to support the business and then give the product away at the end of the day. You are investing very, very large sums of money up front while you have no guarantee that anything ever will come out at the end. That means you have to have high profit leverage, and the higher the leverage the more people are prepared to invest up front in speculative areas. Some areas have produced dramatic breakthroughs. But it is not predictable. You are dealing with biology. Eventually it may be predictable, when we understand more and more about biological control. Today, even with all the knowledge we have, serendipity still plays an enormous role. You know you want to produce good drugs for people, but you also know it is going to cost a hell of a lot of money and time and effort to bring those drugs forward and get them to the people who need them. That means you have to charge reasonable prices for them, and you have to have a monopoly patent otherwise nobody would invest those hundreds and hundreds of millions. When people say, 'Oh, that drug is very expensive' the truth is that drug is extremely cheap if it saves your life. If you have an infection you can either live or die. Take the antibiotic, and you will live. Do not take the antibiotic and you might die. Is £50 to stay alive expensive or is it cheap?

Like everything else in life, it is about behaving in a reasonable manner, getting the balance right, getting the flexibility right, getting the relationships right. If you spend too much time at home you will drive your other half mad. If you spend too much time away you will also drive her mad. It is similar with children. You have to bring children up so they will respect the decision-making process, so they can ask you a question and know they will get a reasonable, balanced answer. Then they can say 'OK. I know I am going to get a reasonable answer. I might not take any notice of it. But at the end of the day I am not going to rail against it, because I have been brought up in an environment that is balanced and where my parents did not say "no, no, no" to everything I asked.'

Of course, with the wisdom of hindsight I wish I had been able to spend more time with the children. Once you have grandchildren you think, 'God, I wish I had spent more time with the children.' But if you lived your life over again you wouldn't. It would be the same. I am absolutely convinced of it. One becomes very sentimental and emotional when you look back, and you never really remember what the hell happened anyway. But you look back and think, 'I should have been there when that happened. I should have been more supportive on this or that occasion.' I am not going to claim that my life was perfect, but I do not think it was very imperfect either.

I think I just about got things right. That may not be the children's perspective. They might say, 'No, no. My father was no role model.' Working as hard as I did creates stresses in any family. The person who felt the stress in my case was my wife, because she was dealing with the kids, she was putting up with me and my problems, she had to make sure meals were ready and everything kept running. So the way you work unintentionally leads to other people's stress. **"**

## Keeping your Balance

- Learn by watching other people. Emulate those you admire, do not model yourself on either the workaholics or slackers.
- When you have been on a long business trip, bring back presents for your family. It shows you have been thinking about them. But you cannot do it on every trip away, and should not even try.
- Think about work problems at home while you are busy doing not much – mowing the lawn or whatever: you will be at work while you are at home, without anyone noticing.

# Chapter 2

## SIR DOMINIC CADBURY

Dominic Cadbury is chairman of the Wellcome Trust and of the
Economist Group, deputy chairman of EMI Group and a director of
Misys. Previously he was chief executive and subsequently chairman of
Cadbury Schweppes, where he spent his career. He is deputy chairman
of the Qualifications and Curriculum Authority and was previously
chairman of the CBI Education Committee. He has recently been
appointed chancellor of Birmingham University.
Dominic Cadbury was born in 1940, educated at Eton College and
Trinity College, Cambridge, and is married with three daughters.


66**W**hat hours does one actually work? When does one actually stop working? I am not a particularly good sleeper
and so I might be working in the middle of the night, because I have
woken up and cannot go back to sleep again. Formally, I have never

been somebody who kept particularly long hours. I was in the office broadly at 8.30 a.m. and never liked to stay beyond six o'clock at night. I did not work longer than that in the office, but the danger is you take work home, stuff papers in your bag and then go on and do extra time when you get back. That is why it is so difficult to know what hours you actually work.

Now I am out of the firing line, in that I am no longer responsible for a public company. From a personal point of view I wanted to free myself up so I would be able to have a life that would offer me the opportunity to do the things I had not been able to do, with all the responsibilities I had before – to achieve a better balance. The opportunity to make more of my private life figured pretty prominently in my decision to retire from Cadbury Schweppes.

At Cadbury Schweppes I worked some part of almost every weekend. The question for me – and it is still a question because I have made the mistake, which almost everybody makes, of taking on too many things for my post-main-job career, if that is the right description – the question is 'How much of the weekend do you give over to work?' I still have to work at the weekends, as I have always done. I could not have done my jobs without it, and still would find it difficult to do the various jobs that I do without working at weekends. The important thing is always to be on the watch at the weekend for those times when it is important to put the work to one side, and be available and free to do other things. The great danger, again, is that you take work home with you and it is so easy, if you are not careful, to sit down and keep doing what you were doing Monday to Friday, only you are at home instead of in the office.

I was always very conscious that work should not invade my private life to the point where it was going to mean my private life became undermined or prejudiced. My private life – primarily my family life – was always too important to me to allow that to happen. I was disciplined about that. Whatever else I did, I was not going to allow my private life to be wrecked by my business life.

My wife always kept the pressure on me, in a pleasant way, not to allow me to sit down at the desk and churn away hour after hour at home. There would always be the caustic comment 'Back to your desk again, I suppose' and that shrewdly reminded me, when I needed to be reminded, that it was better to put the papers away, to stick them back in the briefcase. She was no pushover, in terms of me saying 'Don't bother me this weekend – I am working'. That was not on. She would have blown up and she would have been right to blow up, and I knew it. So I knew the limits I could take things to. She laid down the limits quite cleverly – one could not define the exact parameters, but I knew how far I could take things. And from time to time I would talk over business problems with her. The problems were almost always people problems, because the people problems are the things that keep you awake at night, and the people problems are the ones about which you cannot pretend to your wife that you are not worried – however much you try. She knows darn well that you are worried, and in my case she almost always knew the people. I could always say to my wife, 'I'm bothered about something' and if it was that bad we would have a chat about it.

I never fooled myself that I could unwind completely. Unwinding is not one of my strengths. I am just not very good at it. If I am not worrying about something, I am worried about the fact that I am not worrying about something. I am not one of those people – I do not know how many there are, but I am sure they exist – in the happy situation of just being able to switch off. I have never been able to do that. Switching off takes time. I could always tell you where I was in the process – after three days I was better than after two days. I can switch off progressively on holiday, and I am better on Sunday than I am on Saturday or at the end of the week.

My holidays were not interrupted as a rule, but inevitably there were occasional times when things were happening and I would have to either take a couple of days out of the holiday or cut it short by a day or two. It was not a frequent problem because when I took a holiday I said, 'Right. This is holiday and I do not want to be dragged back into work.' Still, sometimes I had to fly home, and sometimes I knew that before I went. If there was a board meeting or something which I really had to go to, I would come home for a couple of days, and that is not too difficult when you are on the Continent.

Fortunately I cannot remember a major accident situation when I had to drop everything and rush off. I tried to plan as best I could so that for important dates, like meetings with teachers at the children's schools, I made the time available. I managed to do that pretty well. That was helped by working with a company like Cadbury's. The company did not revolve around just me and, while it required me on a full-time basis, it is the kind of company where other people are always capable of keeping everything moving along.

I do not want to sing the praises of the company I spent my life at, and was very committed to, and think very highly of, but the fact is it was the sort of company – it is still the sort of company – where there is an interest in your personal life, in the sense that you should have a personal life that is sensible. Other people rally round if anyone has personal difficulties. We were the sort of company where it was quite easy to go and talk to somebody about such difficulties. If anyone had personal problems the company was always very understanding, and the way the company was organised and managed made it much easier. And the business we were in allowed people to have a more ordered life than, for example, they might have in investment banking. I have never been an investment banker, but I look at them and think, 'Would I really want to follow that sort of life?' Working in investment banking means you are at the end of the phone, the client calls and says, 'I am bidding for . . .' or 'I am being bid for . . .' or 'I am doing this deal . . .' and you have to drop everything immediately – come off your holiday instantly or whatever. In that environment it must be far more difficult to have a sensible work/life balance. Cadbury's was, I suspect, one of the best places you could work, if that really mattered to you, and it did really matter to me.

It had always been in the Cadbury background. My grandfather's vision, which was unique at the time, in creating and developing the Bourneville Village was that a business would be much more likely to succeed if all those who worked in it enjoyed a meaningful and comfortable family life at home away from work. Incidentally in my grandfather's time married women were not employed at Cadbury's, on the basis that when they married they would not be able to combine full-time work with managing the home. Part of the working week at Bourneville, at least for 16 to 18 year-olds, was set aside for classes and education, and this together with further adult education was a passion for my grandfather.

By establishing and developing the Bourneville Village outside Birmingham under the ownership of a trust, not the company, he channelled his business success into improving the lives of the working people, and not just those who worked for Cadbury's. With that kind of heritage and example bequeathed to us, it would be a pretty good disgrace if Cadbury Schweppes, of all companies, didn't have a culture that understood the importance of a sensible work/life balance.

So learning how to keep a balance and a sense of perspective was something that was bred into me. On the way up I had a number of very good people that I worked for, and it was not a surprise to them if I wanted to talk about a personal situation. In many working environments that might be a surprise, or it might even be thought wimpish if you wanted to talk about a personal problem. It was not like that at all in the atmosphere of Cadbury's. It was almost assumed that there would be times when you would want to talk about a personal matter. It was not exactly paternalistic, but the background was. To be modern and contemporary we did not want to be branded as paternalists. So the company moved away – and had already started to move away even before I arrived there – from a paternalistic approach. The danger was that if we took too much interest in people's personal lives, employees would feel they should not be divorced or drink too much or whatever. The Quaker background was powerful. Had we allowed people's personal lives to be of too much interest to the company, we would have become dangerously old-fashioned. At the same time, the door was always open for people to discuss their problems if they wanted to.

Everybody else thinks that the modern way – the right way – is for companies to get more and more involved in people's personal lives. But that is probably because they come from the polar opposite position. Cadbury's is a very long-standing company with a long history. So it is perhaps not surprising that we have been coming at things from almost the other extreme. Arguably, in the 1950s and 1960s, we were too much involved in people's lives, and in the need for them to have, so to speak, healthy private lives. Maybe we went too far. It is a difficult balance for a company to get right.

Travel is a strain, and too much travel undoubtedly makes things very, very difficult because when you are away you are away, and there is not much you can do about it. You can get on the phone and I always used to try to keep in touch on the phone. I did not like to let a day go by, wherever I was in the world, without getting on the phone to home. But that is only a rather small help. The weekends are the critical thing. Can you organise things so as to be back for the weekend, and preferably get back on a Friday? On long trips I found it difficult to get back before Saturday, and would get back Saturday lunchtime or whatever. I was sometimes away for weekends, but I was very conscious that it was pushing things if I ran up too many weekends. That seemed to me to be a real strain on the balance between the family life, the personal life and the working life. So I would try to avoid it as much as I possibly could. I did not always succeed, but it was usually possible to be back home for at least part of the weekend.

I do not think getting home meant I was making sacrifices from the business point of view. Things like conferences in the USA did take place partly over the weekends. You had no choice; you had to be there. But those kind of events often allowed you to have your wife with you. That makes it easier. But in general I was not sacrificing the business in order to be home at the weekend.

The most difficult situation in which I found myself, and in which other people often find themselves, arose because we did not want to live in London, and from about 1983 I was working in London. My background is in the Midlands, my family come from the Midlands, and we did not want to move close enough to

London to make it possible for me to go backwards and forwards to London every day. My difficulty was how to handle life during the week, and how to be home from time to time during the week. If I was not careful I could be sleeping in London for the four nights Monday to Thursday, and only be home Friday, Saturday and Sunday nights. I would be apart from the family throughout the week and then try to make it up over the weekend.

Then I made the mistake of sleeping above the office. The company had very comfortable flats above its offices. I have a small house in London, but I said to myself, 'There is not much point in staying in the house because I can rent it out and sleep in a nice flat, just above work. I have only got to get in the lift and go upstairs and I am home.' You took your papers in the lift and whereas you had been working in your office, you were now working upstairs. Why go to the trouble of going a few miles across London? It is not that much trouble, but it is more trouble than going a couple of floors up in the lift. Why not simply live above the shop? But when my wife and family stayed in the flat with me they did not feel at home. Not in the way that I did. I knew everybody from work, and the security people were people I saw every day, so it seemed perfectly homely to me. Not to them. There was a video camera along the passage to see that there were no intruders, and when my children tore up and down the passage it was all on film – understandably my family did not feel this was much like home. For me it felt very comfortable and it had a nice view out over the park. That did not cut much ice.

It was terribly convenient and in the end disastrously wrong. That was an occasion when my wife put a lot of pressure on me. At first I resisted and said, 'This is how I want to do it.' Then – I do not think it was related to work at all – I got quite seriously ill, and

I agreed to live in my house in London as opposed to the flat above the office. I did it reluctantly, but without any question it was the right thing to do. The inconvenience of going home to my house was trivial compared with the important advantage of getting out of the workplace. Living in the house, my wife was perfectly happy to come to London a couple of nights a week, so we were not separated from Monday to Friday. Even now I have commitments that keep me in London so I cannot go home, and I find myself often in London from Monday night through till Thursday night. My life is easier and I can get home more often. I can get an earlier train and get back OK. But getting the balance right is still a bit of a problem.

I am really a people person, and for that reason the family and friends have featured very prominently in my priorities. In private life we do keep very much in touch with friends, partly through sport, partly through fixing to meet up in the evenings and have dinner together and that sort of thing. My old friends are very old friends. They are people I knew at school. People at university are still good friends too, and that has always meant a lot to me. That is one way in which working in London is quite a bonus, because a number of them are in London – often without their wives during the week – and so we quite frequently get together to either simply have dinner, or in my case I like playing bridge and Monday evenings I play bridge with some of my oldest friends from university.

I play golf, play tennis, go shooting during the winter. Sport is a big interest. I have managed to continue to keep those things going because I really wanted to. The more you really want to do something, the more you are prepared to say, 'No, I am off now. I'm going to go and do it.' The nature of my job and the nature of the company's business being pretty predictable – the chocolate and drinks businesses are pretty predictable businesses – it was easier to fit those things into the diary. By planning them I would know for weeks ahead that 'Right, that's something I'm going to do'. The area that is most difficult to keep up with – you can do things like booking the theatre well ahead – is reading. I suppose if I was a really avid, addicted, reader then I would probably find time to do it. It is so easy to find you are reading, reading, reading lots of business bumph, so that when you sit down to read a book it is quite hard. That is something I miss most, and that I have done the worst. Holidays are fine, you take the books with you and you are jolly well going to read them, and I do. But I find it difficult at the weekend to sit down and read books in the way that I would like to.

E-mails, faxes and so on do not intrude on my private life at all. My business e-mails go to my e-mail address in the office. If I was still in the hot seat at Cadbury's then they might intrude, but I am not. So maybe it is an age thing. They have come at the end of my career rather than the beginning, and e-mail is a wonderful way to keep in touch with my children when they are in other parts of the world. To be able to fire e-mails backwards and forwards across the world has been a wonderful boon. And the mobile phone has made it easier to keep in touch with them because you can ring them and if they are not in their flats, which they are probably not, you have some sort of chance of catching up with them later. So for me all that has been an advantage rather than a disadvantage.

I go to church, partly because it is very local and so there is a local community side to it. I decided fairly late in life to get confirmed, mainly because I was going to church and I did not see why I was only a partly paid-up member. I decided I would like to be fully paid-up. So I became confirmed, and indeed baptised. But my faith is not that strong. I cannot really categorise myself as a committed Christian. The thing that is interesting to me about going to church – and it is a sort of practical approach – is that it is a good time to take the unwinding further. Whenever I do go – and I do not go every Sunday but I go at least every month – it brings a certain relaxation. You think about other things than the thoughts that most intrude on you. I can handle worry because I am used to it, but one of the ways to avoid worrying is to put your mind onto other things. So whether it is going to the theatre or reading a book, playing a game of bridge or going to church, it is, partly, for relaxation. I think about other things and find that comforting.

I believe I worked for a company that behaved responsibly, that provided good careers, good employment. There was – using the jargon in the most general sense – a lot of job satisfaction. I have never doubted that the company and the work were worthwhile. It is easy to trivialise it and say, 'Well, it's just a bar of chocolate', but an awful lot went into that bar and into doing it right, in the right way. The company could not have survived and prospered for as long as it has with brand names that are respected – as they must be if people are going to buy them – if there was not something really worthwhile about it all. And I have done other things that have used my business experience in the public sector, because I thought that they too were worthwhile jobs to do.

Unquestionably I have enjoyed my working life. Enjoying my work has been a great blessing. I almost could say I have enjoyed every single day. The worry is part of the enjoyment. It stimulates me. I am now in a different world, here at the Wellcome Trust. It is a charity and you would expect there not to be any pressure, but I put pressure on myself all the time, even though I am totally out of having to report to shareholders, and having the City on my back, and having to deal with analysts and the press and all the rest of it. I still get a buzz from what I do and I get nervous before I have to do important things. If you are going to do them well, you need to have that touch of excitement and danger, whatever you like to call it. Overall I am more relaxed, admittedly. I am more relaxed but I am certainly not laid back about the jobs I do now. They are important and they have to be done right. You have good times and bad times, but you need the bad times to keep the pressure on yourself, and to keep you finding solutions to things, so even the bad times are good.

I do not think of myself as really ambitious. I was ambitious to run Cadbury's, and I felt sure I could do it. But I do not think I had blind ambition. I felt I could run it successfully if I was given the opportunity, so I was ambitious to be given that opportunity. And then, when I was running the business, I was ambitious to succeed so that people would not say, 'Well, you know, he was just a Cadbury and so of course he got the job of running the business.' I wanted to gain respect for having done the job well, so that I had earned it and deserved it. Maybe behind that was the feeling that because you were in a business with a family name – although it was a completely publicly owned company – people would always say, 'You were only in the job because of who you were.' That drove me to prove myself a bit more than some other people might be driven, because they would not have that same pressure on them.

I hope it does not sound complacent, but looking back I do not think I would have done things differently. My wife would prob- ably disagree, but that would be part of the little pressure that she keeps on me. I have been very lucky to have been in a business and an industry which in my view made it all possible. Questions young people need to give more thought to than perhaps they naturally would, are 'What sort of career do you want to follow? Are you going into a career which will allow you to achieve a sensible balance?' Some careers make it almost impossible. I feel quite sorry for people that I see doing important jobs, but jobs that make it almost impossible for them, however much they try, to get the balance right. It was much, much easier for me. **"**

## Keeping Your Balance

- If you work in London but live too far away to commute every night, as soon as you can afford it get somewhere in town where your wife and children can occasionally come and stay.
- If you live far away from the town where you work and frequently have to stay there overnight, instead of working late each evening make a point of arranging to see your friends – many of whom will, like you, find themselves alone and footloose during the week.
- Even if you have the opportunity, be wary of living above the shop. It sounds wonderfully tempting but it makes the separation of work and private life infinitely more tricky.

# Chapter 3

## MICHAEL GRADE, CBE

Michael Grade is chairman of Pinewood and Shepperton Studios, of the Camelot Group and of Hemscott. He is a director of Charlton Athletic. He is chairman of the Development Council of the Royal National Theatre and on the council of the Royal Albert Hall, a trustee of the Writers and Scholars Educational Trust and a council member of LAMDA. He was formerly chief executive and chairman of First Leisure, chief executive of Channel 4, director of programmes at BBC TV, controller of BBC1, director of programmes at LWT and a theatrical agent and journalist. He has been chairman of the Working Group on the Fear of Crime and a member of the National Committee for the Prevention of Child Abuse. Michael Grade was born in 1943 and educated at St Dunstan's College, has been divorced twice and is now married to his third wife. He has two sons and one daughter.

**66**The pressures on any senior executive in a listed company today are almost unbearable. You have the pressure of the financial press, you have shareholder pressure, you have boards, you have corporate governance. The external pressures, the coverage that you get, is endless – never mind running the business. Then there are trade associations, there is politics – more or less, depending on what business you are in, but inevitably there is some legislation or something that is coming out, an OFT (Office of Fair Trading) enquiry or something from Europe. You could work 24 hours a day and never sleep. You have to be a good delegator. If you are not, I doubt you could keep your sanity.

And that goes a long way to stop you having any personal life at all. So every now and again you have to take time and make time – you absolutely have to. My late father was brilliant. He ran his own business and was his own master (although his was a listed company for a short time). While he was building his business, and even right to the end, when the clock struck six – he could be in the middle of a meeting – he was gone. He went home. And people said, 'But Leslie . . .' and he said, 'I'm off.' He put his coat on and he went. He would leave a roomful of people, in the middle of a deal – anything – and just go. That was his discipline. When he got home he was on the phone all night doing business, but that too was part of his discipline.

There are two major influences in all this. One is the choices that you make yourself about how you manage your time and what is important to you. The other, crucially, is the kind of person your partner is, assuming you are married and have kids. Some partners are more needy than others. Some are working themselves, some are not. In most cases – not all cases – that die is cast, that partnership is cast before you know how far up the greasy pole you are going to get. Many partnerships come to grief because they start out as long weekends together, with every evening at home or going out and doing this and that together. Then, as one partner or the other gets higher up the greasy pole and the demands get greater, the other one gets left behind in terms of attention. That can be very damaging.

I try to keep my wife in touch with what I am doing in business – if not with the detail with the big issues, what I am struggling with, what I am trying to do – in sort of headline terms, so that she does not feel that it is a part of me she cannot reach. I do not do it enough but I do it a hell of a lot more than I used to, and I think that is good. She accepts the situation. She asks, 'Well, why are you doing that?' and I say, 'I've been dealing with it all day. I can't go through it again. Trust me. That is the way it has to be and we have to delay things another six weeks. It means we can't go on holiday.' 'OK, fine.' But at least she does feel involved in the excitements and the ups and downs of what is going on, and that is very helpful.

I have never had an uninterrupted holiday. Never. I did a presentation to the Royal Bank of Scotland about the Pinewood/ Shepperton business standing on a beach in the Maldives with a seaplane waiting to take us to the airport. It was a half-hour question-and-answer session in shorts on the Maldives beach. I went sailing in Turkey when I was at Channel 4 – it was before the really effective GSM mobile stuff, so phoning was difficult then – and we popped into some little port in Southern Turkey. It was a brand new marina and I saw a dialphone and thought, 'My chance to ring the office.' I ring the office, speak to my PA, get through easily – wonderful – and she says, 'The finance director wants to talk to you.'

'Oh fine, OK,' I say. 'Hi, what's going on?'

'I am afraid I've got some bad news for you.'

'What's that?'

'We lost £6 million in the collapse of BCCI last night.'

'Oh! Right! Well, ring the chairman, inform the audit committee, and we'll deal with it when I get back.'

When I got back to the boat, everybody with me in Turkey looked at me as if there had been a death in the family.

'What happened?'

'We've just done 6 million quid in cold blood in BCCI.'

We were down in Cornwall this year for two weeks, a family holiday, nice house on a beach, and I had to come back for my BBC chairmanship interview in the middle of the holiday. I did not even expect to get the job. And I didn't.

My wife copes with all that – with difficulty. She is very understanding but she would much rather it did not happen. And I would much rather it did not happen. What I do try to do to compensate is have lots of treats. On Thursday I am taking her to New York. Her brother is working there. I said, 'Let's go to New York, do a bit of shopping. We'll go and see Mel Brooks' *The Producers*. I have a couple of tiny bits of business to do there as well. I don't have to do them, but I can do them while we are there. But we will take four days off.' So I keep having little treats. We go off here, we go off there.

The first question I asked my present wife when I met her was whether she liked sailing or not, whether she had ever even been sailing. She said her sister's partner had a boat and sailing was one of her great thrills. She loved it. I thought 'I'm in here – we'll be all right then.' Sailing is a passion. I had a boat, she loved sailing, and it is something you can do together. You can even sleep together doing it. You have a cabin – it is like a country cottage.

And there are other things we share, and that is important. She loves music, I love music so we can sit and listen to CDs of an evening, or a concert on the radio – wonderful. We go to the National Theatre a lot – I do some work for the National so we get to go quite a bit. We go to movies – like me she loves the movies. Sailing – when I had a boat – movies, music, theatre, and skiing once a year, she likes skiing too. We are very compatible. The only bone of contention at the weekends is football. That's a passion too. She does come occasionally. She drags herself because she feels she ought to, but it is a duty thing. She doesn't really get it.

Weekends I like to spend at home – apart from when I go to football, that is. My idea of a night out is to go home and have a meal in front of the television with my wife and watch a movie or programme together. That is my idea of bliss. Or we go to the theatre, just her and me, or the movies or something. That is bliss too. I do not play golf anymore. I used to when I was younger. When I was married to my first wife I played a lot of golf, and that is totally anti-social because you are out pretty well all day.

I have not got many really old friends – nobody has – but I have got a circle of friends going back 20 or 30 years. I am very careful about making friends in business. You must be careful not to mix friendship and business without thinking about it very carefully, to be absolutely sure that you really like the person and that your partners get on. You have to be quite calculating about it before you dive in too deeply on the social side. And I have a thing about neighbours. I would rather have a reputation for being stuck up than find myself trapped. I have to spend enough time with enough people I do not particularly like. So you have to manage things.

You have to be absolutely brutal. It has taken me years to get to this state of grace but I am absolutely ruthless about it now.

Some of the companies I have worked for have understood the work/life balance thing, some have not. I myself have made it a rule as a manager to be very family-friendly. I send people home. 'Go home. Just go and look after him', or 'If you've got a problem at home, just go.' Family comes first. If somebody comes in and says, 'Look, I am really sorry. You know you've got this urgent all-day strategy meeting. Is it all right if I come for half a day?'

'What's the problem?'

'Well, the wife's going into hospital . . .'

'Don't come for half a day, just go home.'

Family must come first. I have always been very anxious for staff who work for me to feel that. And as far as people I have worked for, if I have thought it was important for me to attend a family matter I would not have any compunction. If anybody did not like it, tough. That is the package.

I like to be at important meetings myself because I am a control freak, but at the end of the day, if the wife is locked out and the child is crying and I am the only one with the key, it's, 'Sorry, guys.' That is if there is a personal crisis, if there is something that cannot be done by somebody else. I have learned this only slowly; it comes with a state of security about your own career. When you are insecure it's; 'I can't leave. Otherwise it will all happen without me . . .' Insecurity is a great motivating dynamic but it can also be very destructive. And when I was younger I felt it. But I always tried to make parents' evenings, and things like that. I have flown back from abroad for parents' evenings. And when you are fairly high up in a company you should have some pretty good people around you to whom you can say, 'Look, I've got to leave this to you. Call me if there's a problem, or I'll phone you at nine o'clock tonight.'

I have always had very strong one-on-one relationships in all my business life. When I was at the *Daily Mirror* it was with another fellow journalist who was very experienced and taught me the ropes. When I went into show business I worked with a man called Billy Marsh who I had a very, very close working relationship with. At London Weekend Television I worked with Cyril Bennett and John Freeman, and then Brian Tessler. When I went to California it was the same. And when I got back here it was the same again at the BBC and at Channel 4. I have had patrons all along the line. I respected them and they must have respected me. In my working life I have always been very careful to choose who I work for, and that has paid off. I have learned wonderful things about managing life, from great teachers.

I learned how to deal with committees too. You cannot have two more bureaucratic organisations than the old federal system of ITV, and the BBC. The ITV network federal system was like operating in Brussels in the EC. When I left London Weekend in 1981 I was on 29 ITV committees. You had to know how to work those committees to make sure that London Weekend got what it wanted. They all had a purpose. They were not just talking shops. And at the BBC everything is done by committees. Nothing happens without a committee. So I am quite used to the corporate insti-tutionalised way of working. And having to be at them. And the time it all takes.

It sounds stressful, but it has not been. I have never found work stressful – tiring, yes. Brief moments of stress, perhaps: 'How is this one going to work out?' But the only night's sleep I ever lose at work is when I know I have to fire somebody the next day. I do

not lose sleep over deals – 'Will it work out? Won't it work out?'
'The ratings are up, the ratings are down' – things like that do not
stress me. I need to relax, yes. Stress, no. Apart from firing people
the only thing that can make me feel really stressed is office politics. So I have avoided them like the plague. Always. That is what
drove me out of the BBC in the end. I have only ever been in a
situation twice where I have had real office politics to deal with.
One was at the BBC, and the other was towards the end at First
Leisure. The board got political and I did find that a bit stressful. I
have not got the patience for office politics. They are so unpro-
ductive. It does not sell more widgets. It does not increase your
margins. It is just energy-sapping. So avoid them. Then – if you are
lucky enough to be in businesses that you are quite good at and
that you actually enjoy – business is fun.

As soon as I get up every morning I go into work mode. When I
wake up I get very distracted and my wife cannot get through to
me. She says, 'I just asked you whether you . . .' 'Oh sorry darling,'
I reply absent-mindedly. I am processing stuff. 'What do I need to
do today? What is coming to the surface? Oh hell, I know what I've
got to do . . . I really must get on with that today.' I spend half an
hour or an hour working out the day's stuff that needs to be done.
I am a pretty instinctive person, but what informs my instinct is
thinking around problems. In two weeks' time I have to make a
speech that I can only write myself. And in spare moments I will
make a few notes as I am thinking about it, and then by the night
before it is more or less there. I work with a notebook now, which
I rather like. I jot down things I need to do, things people have
said, phone numbers, and I work through them later. I got that
from Richard Branson. I had several meetings with him years ago
and he had this little school exercise book and kept writing in it

and reading it. Then he would say, 'Well, last time, Michael, you said . . .' I thought, that's a good system. I use that system constantly now that I am no longer a full-time executive – with one business and one support system – and as I go from business to business I keep notes in my book.

Things can be made more problematic by all the new communications aids. You have to be careful you are not loading yourself up with more and more information that you are unable to process effectively and thoughtfully, as well as instinctively. The danger is you have a fax machine in the car, two telephones and e-mail and all that: when do you get thinking time? And you really, really have to make sure you have thinking time. I look at e-mails at the weekend and every evening when I get home. And I take business calls whenever, if people need to ring me. As a chairman, people do not waste your time, fortunately. The chief executives have not got time to waste themselves. If I start to get too many phone calls from one of my chief executives, I start to wonder if are they losing the plot.

I come from a successful family where my father and his two brothers all turned out to be wizards at the same business, and I ended up going into that same business. So my career has been totally important to me – a self-imposed burden, a motivating force. All along the way I made the choices. I could have been a happy beach bum and not starved, but my choice has been to have a career. My family never said to me, 'Michael, you've got to succeed.' Never. 'Be happy, Michael. Do whatever you want to do,' they said. There was never any pressure to achieve, not from the family. It was purely self-imposed and it has been both very constructive and very destructive in different ways. Second-best will not do for me. It is not based on the amount of money you make –

you just have to do a good job and keep moving forward and upwards. That has always been my priority. That is what has driven me for 30-odd years and it has taken its toll. I have been married three times. And there is no question that was partly, at least, the result of business pressures. When I was younger and my wife complained about how much time I spent working, I ignored it. I was too busy even to think about the relationships I got into. I did not ask, 'Am I absolutely sure?' I thought, 'Don't worry, it will be fine. Let's get married.' And then the marriages did not stick – two of them did not stick. The third one has, because I learned from the other two.

I do not want to be king of the world or richer than Croesus. Whatever I decide I want to do, I want to be the best at it. If that means I have to work harder than anybody else because I am not that good at it, I will do whatever it takes. Fear of failure has now receded, because you get to a point where you have built up certain good-will, you have secure judgment and you know when to leave things alone and to take a day off, or whatever. You know your career is not going to come to an end if you take a day off.

I am not sure whether things have changed over the years. For younger executives I do not think an awful lot has changed. At that age it is a question of how much pressure you put on yourself to perform. Where do you want to get? Do you want to be a captain of industry? Are you happy to settle for less? Are you going to squeeze every ounce out of the job so that you can go off and start your own business in five years' time? What is your goal? Once you get to the boardroom, or the edge of the boardroom, then things change. The time pressures just grow and grow. People say 'Oh, we never see our chairman or chief executive in the factory.' So you have to go and meet the staff, you have got to walk the floor.

It takes time. You have to keep consulting, carry the people with you. You have to manage every change – trying to persuade people it is a good thing to move from the third floor to the seventh floor. Hours and hours of meetings, of talking. When you get home you are talked out. By the time I get home I do not want to say another word or make another decision. My wife is worrying about choosing a school, or 'Which wallpaper do you think?' or 'Where do you want to go on holiday?' – 'Oh, don't ask me to make another decision!' She understands now that when I get home I need half an hour – that is all it takes – to unload and reboot, or unboot really. I switch off and then I am fine and up and running again.

Looking back, I do not know if I could have managed things better. The only thing I could have done is not have allowed myself to have been so driven, to live up to the family tradition. If I had made that choice much earlier I might well have done better at family life earlier, I do not know. It was a kind of spiral because if my work had not been going well while my personal life was in a bit of a mess, I think I would have lost my sanity. Work was a refuge from problems at home and I would throw myself more and more into work, and into the success I had at work. That was why I didn't listen when my wife told me to let up on work a bit. That way you could deal with the fact that you had an unsuccessful private life, which itself was partly caused by the work. The two things fed off each other. It was a pinball, ping-pong thing.

I started off by wanting to be successful and to work very hard. As a result of that, I screwed up two marriages. But the fact that work was going well enabled me to get through. I was getting my fulfilment from work. I wasn't at home. There is no blame here on anybody but myself. I was too busy even to be stressed. There was no time. You block it all out and throw more work in – another pile of programme cassettes to watch, scripts to read, budgets to look at, TV to watch at night to see what the opposition is doing. 'Oh is that a new show starting at midnight? Then I don't have time to go to bed.' It was a good escape. I was in a business that was open 24 hours a day.

I do not think my present wife would have been interested in me if she had met me 20 years ago. She is much younger than I am, and if she had met me then I do not think we would have lasted five minutes. She would not have put up with me the way I was. I am still not great, but I am better because I have been through it. You get a much better sense as you get older of what is and is not important in life, both at work and at home.

Your children suffer – probably more than your partner. They do not see their dad. I was very much an absentee father when my oldest children were growing up. I would go to parents' nights and all that but I never felt then that I should spend more time with the kids. I should have done. I was very young. I have made up for it since, I hope. My relationship with the baby now is very different. I often stop when I am playing with him and I think, 'I never did this with the others.' I was on a mission to conquer the world. I am sure they have forgiven me. I do not think they feel particularly hard done by now, because the relationships are strong now.

I have a strong religious faith, which helps me, though I would not say I was a devout practitioner by any stretch of the imagination. I am a classic two or three times a year at the synagogue man. The particular bit of the Jewish church that I belong to – the liberal bit – is very undemanding in terms of ritual and guilt. The usual manoeuvres that religions use to control their flock are not much in evidence. It is stripped down to the basics of faith, which I rather like. I cannot be doing with the control mechanisms of the different groups that seem to have nothing to do with true religion at all. Perhaps enjoy is the wrong word, but I do actually enjoy Yom Kippur, spending three or four hours at a stretch at the synagogue. I find it good to just stop. It is a time for thought.

I have always regarded work as my mistress and whoever my partner has been, they have had to understand. The fact was that the mistress had an aerial and was plugged into the wall and had a video machine underneath, but essentially my partners always had to share me with my mistress, my work. **99**

## Keeping Your Balance

- Try hard to find a partner who shares your hobbies and interests. This may sound impossibly cold and clinical, but if you get it wrong you will end up spending your leisure time as well as your work time in separate worlds.
- If you need time to unwind when you first get home of an evening, or to wind yourself up in the morning, explain this to your partner. A single explanation will avert a thousand misunderstandings.
- Before turning business acquaintances into personal friends, try to ensure your partners will be friends too. Otherwise your new friendship will become an additional strain on your work/life balance, instead of a helpful additional bond.

# Chapter 4

---

# BARONESS HOGG

Sarah Hogg is chairman of 3i and of Frontier Economics. She is a governor of the BBC and a director of P&O Princess Cruises and GKN. She was formerly a journalist with *The Economist*, *The Times*, the *Independent* and the *Sunday Times* and has been economics editor of *Channel 4 News*, the *Daily Telegraph* and the *Sunday Telegraph*. She was head of the Downing Street Policy Unit from 1990 to 1995. Sarah Hogg was born in 1946, and educated at St Mary's Convent, Ascot, and Lady Margaret Hall, Oxford. She is married to the Rt Hon. Douglas Hogg, QC, MP, and has a son and a daughter.

**"**In many ways balancing your work and your personal life is a lot harder than it was when I started work. The work pressures on people are so much greater. Looking at both my children, I see the demands on people starting out on their careers to be much greater than they were. They work far longer hours than I did in my twenties, so it is a lot tougher for them than it was for me.

The more I look back on my working life, the more convinced I am of my dependence on good fortune. If you are working and bringing up a family, having luck, in terms of one's children's health and the general ability to run one's life on a continuing basis, without having to drop everything and concentrate exclusively on them – and I was well aware at all points that something could easily happen that would mean I would have to do that – was just very fortunate.

It would be wrong to say that I was conscious of a clash between my work and my family, though I was always aware that there was the potential for a clash. Everything could be balanced but if something went seriously wrong with my children – the most obvious thing a working mother thinks of – then there would be a clash. It would not really have been a clash, as it was entirely clear in my mind which way it would be resolved. I would drop everything for my children. So in that sense it was not stressful. There was no worrying about the decision. It was clear which way the decision would go. But one never stops being aware that the potential for a problem, a clash, is out there.

A new colleague had just arrived to join *The Economist* from the Bank of England when one of my children went down with measles and I had to stop work and cancel the children's party. Not much of a clash perhaps – a trivial event compared with the things that people have to cope with in balancing these things. But having to share a room with a mother who has to make 30 calls to other mothers talking about measles probably brought the work/life balance forcibly home to him, if not to me. I must have driven him completely mad, though despite that he still remains a great friend! There was another kind of clash – I was mortified because it appeared in a newspaper diary story somewhere – when I was out in Japan with a bunch of economic journalists. We were due to interview the Japanese Prime Minister and he wanted to change the day of the interview from Tuesday to Friday. This would have meant I could not get back for half-term. I went on and on and on at the Japanese officials until they shunted the interview back to Tuesday again, much to the embarrassment of the others in our delegation.

I was very queasy throughout my pregnancies, and sitting through meetings was pretty grim – but that did not involve a choice, you just got on with things. So I do not think I felt stress in the sense of agonising over choices. The stress was that you were always busy, probably ratty, and there was never a time when you could think, 'Ah, I don't have much to do now. This is my time.' But full-time mothers have exactly that experience too, so I do not think stress was any worse for me than for women who are full-time mothers – which is itself a pretty stressful activity.

And we did not work such long hours then as people work now. During the first period of my children's life I was working at *The Economist*, which had a heavy work peak in the middle of the week. We worked very, very late on Wednesday night but that was only one night a week, and it seems to me there are lots of people in their twenties and thirties now working until two or three in the morning many nights a week. What is more, they do not know which nights it is going to be. Most personal systems can cope with regular pressure points but it is the irregular ones – the sudden demands to do this by three o'clock in the morning – that put pretty intolerable pressure on the patterns and structures that people develop for themselves.

The only job I had when it was really necessary to be on call – on demand 24 hours a day, seven days a week, just about every day of the year – was my 10 Downing Street job in the Cabinet Office, and by then my children were already grown up so there was not quite the same pressure. One newspaper diary story that got published while I was working in Downing Street said that I had rushed home from something important to look after my young children. My 'young children' were by that stage 21 and 18. *The Times* did apologise!

Throughout the time I was working I had help at home, and I was very lucky in the quality of help I had. And I was lucky in earning enough to be able to afford it. When my daughter was born I remember talking to Lady Plowden, who had just produced a great report on nursery education, and she said, 'Never think it is easy to find a substitute for yourself.' It is a very important principle. My first piece of good fortune was that the nanny who brought me up for the first four years of my life came back and started me off, and indeed was in and out of our house for a long time afterwards, filling gaps when she had partially retired. I was perhaps the last generation to have the benefit of those wonderfully devoted people who gave their whole lives to looking after children. Though I will not say she deeply approved of working mothers; she would 'tut tut' frightfully about it. On the other hand, I had total confidence in her. Then I had a brilliant Norland-trained nanny. She was devoted to the children. I myself was brought up in a convent so I am a boarding school child, and both my children were boarding-school children, which clearly took quite a lot of the load off me in their upbringing period but, looking back on it, was exceedingly good in terms of the quality of upbringing delivered to the two of them. Their schools did a lot for them. I am very grateful for that.

Work sometimes interfered with holidays, though that probably happened more because of my husband being called back for one thing or another. Being in politics, his own life provided those unexpected crises at double strength. So most of our holiday cancellations have been because of his return to parliament, having to get back for a vote or something, much more than my work. I am only beginning to realise now, as I get older, that holidays were not that restful because I wanted to spend all my holiday time with my children. We hardly ever got away on our own, and I think that was a pity. Now it is a delight, a rediscovery, for just the two of us to be going away.

As a working mother I felt relatively unusual when the children were young. I did not feel glamorously pioneering in any way. There were more and more women who were pursuing their careers, but at that stage they would usually stop and start again after quite a long chunk of time out. So at the time I was unusual in going all the way through, but between the birth of my two children I was running *The Economist* book pages, which was something you could do with a book perched on the swelling tummy and your feet up. I was very lucky to have that job.

Usually the problems of balancing work and family are much worse for women than for men, and for my generation it was even truer than for this generation. For my generation the main day-to-day load – the day-to-day administration of running the home and bringing up the children – fell on the mother rather than the father. At the start of my working life in 1967 there were women I worked with – even at *The Economist*, supposedly quite an advanced institution – who thought that women should stop work when they had children, or even when they got married. There was one woman there – a senior editor – who told me this fiercely. So there was that atmosphere to contend with. Maternity leave barely existed, so I was back in the office three weeks after my daughter was born. Today it is a very different world.

In those days – I hope not now – I think a lot of women lied when they had to have time off for their children, giving some other reason for their absence. Sudden illness, which could be so terrifying in young children, I covered at least once by giving the impression I was ill myself, or at least blurring the distinction. It was not a good idea, because I would then end up working when I really was not well in order to 'make up'; but women of my generation felt vulnerable to those looking for evidence we couldn't combine responsible careers and motherhood. So I reckoned men could take time off with colds but I had to 'bank' time for children's crises – fortunately (luck, again) I had relatively good health. I also had one boss who (bless him) used to send me home whenever he spotted me overcompensating.

I worked for *The Economist* all the time my children were really young and I do not think they gave advice particularly. On the other hand the working environment was pretty relaxed. I was not trying to do an international job at *The Economist*, which would have been much more difficult and demanding. At her leaving party at *The Economist*, one woman said, 'I will never say anything nasty about *The Economist* because on *Economist*-time I wrote three books and had two children.' I myself could not quite claim the same, but there was spare capacity of time that you could use. It was very much more relaxed than most of the jobs I see around me today.

The key thing was that my husband was really, really keen I should stay at work. I would come back and say, 'Oh, perhaps I'll give myself an easier life', because every mother who works has that foolish notion. In fact I do not think being a full-time mother and doing it all myself would have been an easier life at all. In any event my husband would say, 'No, you've got to stick at it', and that meant that he never grumbled when I had to be at work late, because he knew that doing both jobs was important for me. I do not think he would have in any way claimed to be a 'new man' – he didn't change a nappy once – but knowing he would never complain about me being home late because of my work was absolutely vital to me. His psychological commitment and his enthusiastic support gave me the feeling that I was not doing it on sufferance, as many women of my generation were. He even refused to be Paymaster-General because he thought it might conflict with my financial journalism.

His psychological support was more important than his practical support, although he would always plunge in and help in a crisis. If he had actually had to cope with two children under the age of four by himself for any length of time, the phone would have been ringing pretty fast at my mother's, at his mother's, or at anybody else's he could conceivably think of. But the fact that I knew he would grip things and that I could do what I had to and have absolute confidence that he would not grumble was wonderful.

And I would discuss work problems with him a lot. All those classic women's worries, feeling very uncertain all the time and worrying about, 'Am I capable of doing this?' 'Can I do this?' 'I am sure I've got that terribly wrong and this has got to be the end of my entire career' kind of stuff, which I went in for a lot. Being able to bounce things off him was essential.

Like most women of my generation, at work I did feel I had to prove myself in a man's world. It is difficult to disentangle nature, nurture and all the elements of this. I am sure I exhibited the

'You've got to perform doubly well' anxieties. Whether that was because it was an alien or hostile world, or whether it was because I had a convent upbringing and I was always worrying about doing my best and all that, I would not know. I am a workaholic so I would probably feel guilty when I was not working anyway. And work is fun.

I know we did not spend enough time relaxing on our own. Work and children absorbed most of my life. I am sure this generation handles these things much better – I did not find enough time for exercise and sport until recently, and it is very important to your equilibrium. Today they are very much better at keeping fit in their twenties and thirties, but at that age my only exercise seemed to be running for the bus. However, from quite early on in my children's life we were living half in London and half in my husband's constituency so there was fresh air and walks in the country at the weekends. Being out of London is my great detox, and always has been. There is always a lot to do in the country at weekends, because if you are trying to run two places that you live in and you are trying to help your husband in his constituency, you cannot just go there and collapse. Nonetheless the fresh air and the being out of London were tremendously important.

It has all meant I did not manage to keep up with all my friends as much as I would have liked. I am immensely gregarious. I like having lots of friends and it has been very difficult to keep different groups of friends going. I empathise with the issue much discussed now – it was not discussed in my generation but it was still true – that you would seem quite unfriendly at work if you did not stay around and hang around in the pub in the evenings. I think that is a big issue for women, because it is a very important part of the bonding process – and it is especially true in journalism, where

I spent the first chunk of my working career. I would get my work done and run for home, and if you are not careful that leaves a very unfriendly impression. So I gave nurturing friendships at work less time than I would have liked. But keeping up with friends from other groups was very hard too. I still have close friends from school and university, so at least I have hung on to some of them.

And I still have some close friends from each place I worked. But the general bonding with everybody at work – having the wide group of friends at work which is very important in many businesses – that is the bit I am sure I did not do enough of. On the other hand, given the choice again I would do exactly the same, and run for home. That is where the choice between work and family probably hit most obviously. The whole network of work relationships, and being friendly with everybody – that is most difficult to maintain if you are trying to get home and see your children. There is a lot written about it now, and I think this reflects a real problem.

Modern communications – e-mails and mobile phones and the rest – are a huge advantage. Yes they interfere, and yes you know that while you are having a chat, a stack of e-mails is building up. That is a pressure and it means that Sunday evenings are not relaxed fireside occasions any more, but times to try and get that load out of the way so you can start Monday relatively clear. But the huge advantage is being able to manage your life from wherever you are, and develop the essential skill of moving from one subject to another – which also comes from those same communication channels.

Companies are becoming – I was going to say more relaxed, but that is not the right word – becoming more sophisticated about understanding that people can deliver good work remotely. I do not think you can have key management people who never come into the office. That would be unreal. But understanding that you can get good value from somebody spending a day at home and storming through the mental and writing work can be extremely advantageous for a company. Companies being relaxed about that is a big change, and an important one, and very useful for all forms of work.

Companies are also becoming much more understanding of people's problems. The difficulty can still be that they catch up too late – and 'Who's to blame for that?' is a difficult question. Somebody may have gone through a terrible week, but how can you be sure of discovering that without being totally intrusive? That is a real problem. If you hear at the end of the week that somebody's father died ten days ago and that explains a lot of things, are you going to tick people off for not telling you their fathers have died? If they were internalising it and not wanting to shout it around that is their privilege. When alerted to these issues most companies can be pretty good. But it is still a difficult balance, because there can be acute pressure points where a company's livelihood is also at stake, and managing that through periods of personal difficulty in key individuals' lives is not at all easy.

Looking back, I do not think I managed my work/life balance particularly well at all. As I say, I am convinced that if I survived with two wonderful children, it is luck. It is to do with having been fortunate in the jobs I had, and being fortunate in the children's health, and luck in finding good schools, luck in the people who looked after them – luck, luck, all the way along the line. I do not put anything down to good judgment. I think so much of bringing up children is luck anyway and I had a huge dollop of it. But there is a difference between thinking you got things right or wrong, by luck, and feeling guilty about it. To feel guilty I would have needed to feel that I had made a consistent pattern of choices that disadvantaged the children, and that they were wrong choices. I do not think that. But when it comes to 'Did I get things right?', no, I got lots of things wrong. I think getting children's upbringing right is exceptionally difficult, and probably as a parent one gets most of it wrong most of the time!

How you manage these things changes all the time. That is partly cultural, partly the nature of the working environment, so I do not think there are many lessons to be learned from a previous generation. But if you have worked through bringing up your children, that should at least help you understand the balancing act that the next generation is trying to achieve. And it has made me more admiring of them because I think it is a lot harder now than I had to contend with. If it has taught me anything, it is that. **"**

## Keeping Your Balance

- Get away with your partner – without your children – from time to time.
- Finding really good people to look after your children is never easy. Do not skimp on the time and effort required.
- Once you have decided on your priorities, go for them. If that means shifting important meetings or failing to have a drink in the pub of an evening – too bad. Don't agonise over it.
- Times have changed, and it is no longer necessary for women (or indeed men) to blur the issue when they take time off for family reasons. Be totally truthful – both for yourself and for the wider cause of everyone's work/life balance.

# Chapter 5

# LORD MARSHALL

Colin Marshall is chairman (formally chief executive) of British Airways, chairman of Invensys, of the Royal Institute of International Affairs, of the Conference Board, Inc., and of Britain in Europe. He is a director of HSBC Holdings, a member and formerly chairman of the International Advisory Board of the British-American Business Council, a member of the IOD Council and a trustee of the Duke of Edinburgh's UK Leadership Forum. He was formerly president, chief executive and then chairman of Avis, chairman of London First Centre and of the London Development Partnership, deputy chairman of BT, and a director of Grand Metropolitan, Midland Bank, IBM UK, USAir, Quantas and the Business in the Community Women's Economic Development Team. He was a co-founder and chairman of the Marketing Council, president of the Chartered Institute of Marketing, vice-president of the Advertising Association and a member of the Executive Committee of IATA and of the Hong Kong Association. Colin Marshall was born in 1933 and was educated at University College School, Hampstead. He is married and has one daughter.

**"Y**ou cannot separate your work and personal lives, you cannot have a totally independent work life and personal life. In the end, if you really want to be successful, you have to merge the two together, and that means you have to hit the right balance between them. The right balance for you, for anyone, will depend on what your own ambitions are, on your own desires and on what your family's requirements and expectations are as well. That changes as you go through life. At this stage of life my requirements, expectations and desires, and my family's, are quite different from what they were 30 years ago, or maybe even 15 years ago. Given all the pressures that there are in life today – and there are pressures on people's personal lifestyles as well as there clearly are on the work side – getting the balance right can be pretty tough.

Without any doubt companies are more understanding than they were, and that means the individuals running the companies are more understanding. That has occurred inevitably, because those people have come under the same pressures during their careers, and so they have had a much better appreciation of them as they have moved upwards. Today the issue is very important, and generally speaking the more successful companies are the more enlightened companies. Companies that display a real social conscience are generally in the vanguard of success.

I myself do not work to any set timetable at all, other than that I am an early bird. I believe in being in my office by seven o'clock in the morning or shortly thereafter, getting under way immediately. The end of the working day will depend on my having completed all I needed to complete, given my various business interests. That often means going out in the evening, perhaps to a social event with a customer, or being entertained oneself by a supplier or whoever. If I am at home I always have work with me in my briefcase, which I attend to at the first opportunity. I am fortunate in that I have a driver, and with traffic conditions in London and elsewhere these days, I can cover a lot of work, reading business papers, while I am in the car. That saves a lot of time. And the mobile phone enables me to deal with a lot of things first thing in the morning, particularly if I am not coming directly to my office.

There is always some office work to cover at weekends. Generally that involves reading board papers for meetings that are coming up the following week. I encourage companies I am associated with to make sure all board members receive their papers by the previous Friday evening or to have them delivered to their homes on Saturday morning at the latest. Then they have the opportunity to read them in a more relaxed environment – at least hopefully a more relaxed environment – at home, rather than in the busier environment of the office.

Inevitably my holidays have sometimes been interrupted. There have been some absolutely appalling times when that has occurred, but it is part of what you take on if you really want to move up and be successful in business. Not that it only applies in business. It applies in many other fields. It applies to an even greater extent in politics. Anyway I would not say it has happened that often. Over the years I have learned that the most sensible time for me to take a holiday is the second half of August, when business in general quietens down – that is not quite true of the airline business, which is very busy then, but everybody has already booked their flights and there is nothing much more for you to do as a manager. Nonetheless there have been occasions when I have had to fly back from holiday for a board meeting or whatever it might be. And even on holiday there are virtually daily telephone calls.

If you want to be a chief executive, managing director, president, chairman or whatever, you have to accept that you cannot walk away from the business at any time – unless you are quitting! – and when you go on holiday you have to accept that there may be a need for people to speak to you, to check something with you. It is all right saying you will hand the responsibility over to someone else, but in the end you are the one who is going to be held to account if something goes wrong. If the person I have put in charge in my absence feels uncertain about a decision, I would not want that person to go ahead and take the decision without referring back to me first.

With so much happening some stress is inevitable. There certainly have been times where I have felt I was almost drowning, but I have always managed to claw myself back out of the water. Stress is something one has to learn to live with and to deal with sensibly. The most important thing is to get a good night's sleep – at least a few hours of good sleep – and not to go to bed with a whole mass of things on your mind that you are worrying about and that result in you getting only intermittent sleep. That's bad. Fortunately I am able to switch off when I go to bed and generally sleep soundly – it may be only for four and a half or five hours, but at least it is good sleep for that period of time. I can get by on four to five hours' sleep. But I am not one of those people who can switch off during the day, so if I am on a long flight I very rarely if ever doze off – unless it is the normal time to go to sleep, that is.

Sleep is particularly important when you do a lot of travelling, naturally. I have travelled virtually all of my working life. When I left school I did not go to university. I went straight into the Merchant Navy and set off travelling around the world as a cadet, and I have continued to travel ever since. So I have effectively been travelling now for over 50 years. In the past it was a much more sedate form of travel, by ship, which gave you plenty of time to adjust to time zones. With air travel I am one of the lucky ones. Jet-lag does not affect me to any great extent. I long ago determined that when I arrive, wherever it may be, I will go onto local time immediately. If that means having breakfast, have breakfast. If it means having dinner, have dinner. If it means going to bed, go to bed. And I have managed to run my life on that basis. It has caused a degree of fatigue from time to time, particularly if you go from here to Sydney or to Tokyo, and you arrive first thing in the morning their time, and you have a very full day of business to get through, plus a dinner in the evening. By the time you finally get to bed you are a little bit weary! Then you sleep very well and recover.

But doing so much travelling meant my daughter did not see much of me when she was young. I accept that and I guess it is the one regret I have in life. The time that she was growing up, particularly pre-teens, was a time when I was travelling virtually flat out. In one year during that period I was away for about 270 days out of 365. Then we moved to New York when she was just 11 years old, and we gave her the option of coming with us, and going to school in New York, or staying at the prep school she was at already here in England, as a boarder – she was a day-girl up till then – and she elected to stay at the prep school and board. Then she went on to her senior school and then on to university. So I did not see too much of her in those teen years because she was here, we were living in the States, and anyway I was travelling an awful lot. I used to get back to London roughly every six weeks, and I always tried to be here at the end of the week so I could take her out from school on a Saturday afternoon, have dinner with her and then take her back to school while I flew back to New York. But she grew up without my being too obviously around.

Individual families have to determine how they want to play their lives. My wife has been enormously supportive. From day one she has been accustomed to my travelling extensively, so there has never been anything new about that from her standpoint. And she has travelled with me from time to time – not that frequently but maybe two or three times in a year, usually on relatively short trips.

My wife's support has been both psychological and practical – and very important indeed to me. In the earlier days of my working life, the international phone systems were none too hot, which could make it really difficult to keep in touch. These days it is almost instant. Connection is simple to maintain, so I make a point of being in touch with her every day, as far as possible. It is vital for your partner to feel able to have access to you wherever you may be. And from a practical, organisational standpoint you are dependent on your partner being able to manage the home side, the family side and so on. My wife is very good at reminding me of the key things that are extremely important from a family life standpoint.

And there have been crises in my life on two or three occasions when I have had a call from her and have had to drop what I was doing and get onto the next plane home. It is absolutely essential to do that because it is part of the psychological bonding within a family. The companies I worked for have always understood. They have understood that if you were away from home when there was a crisis you would need to rush back immediately. When we got married and emigrated to the United States I went straight into a US-type environment working for a US company, and in those days – we are going back to the late 1950s – American companies were already more enlightened about people's personal lives than people were in England and in many other areas of the world. That probably helped me to mould my own attitudes, and helped me to recognise its importance. Today, in British Airways we have an important HR function, we have people who help with counselling and guidance and with goodness knows what!

Things are even more difficult for women who work than for men. Until it becomes much more accepted that the man in the partnership is going to do the things women have traditionally done, women have to do most of what they have always done, as well as take on the business side. On top of that, women today have to be at least marginally better than their male equivalents, to get the jobs they get. That phenomenon is reducing all the time, but it is still a factor right now.

Virtually all of my business life has been in the service sector, and therefore very people-related. Interpersonal relationships are all-important. I am not particularly conscious of needing time alone. But there are occasions, now at this later stage in life, where on a weekend away from London I enjoy having half an hour or an hour to myself to go for a walk in the country. I still play tennis and really enjoy that. Whenever I am travelling I take a racquet if there is the least chance of getting a game while I am away. So I have played tennis in quite a few countries and in different climates around the world. I try to play once a week, though it probably averages out to maybe three times a month, and it is now my only active sport. But I am an avid sports enthusiast so I love watching rugger and soccer. On the rugger side I am a great Twickenham-goer. I am a season-ticket holder at Highbury and have been a life-long Arsenal supporter. I love American football too, and love to watch the World Series baseball whenever I get the chance.

I have always been ambitious to get on, to achieve, and that equates to being successful. But from my standpoint I wanted just to feel that I was really achieving something in life – not necessarily specifically for myself, not necessarily for the family, but to achieve it for the company that I was working for, was involved with, and to see that benefit reflected in the organisation itself. Nor has it really been for money. I have always left it entirely to those who have had the responsibility for doing so to determine what I should get. I have never asked for any specific amount of money, nor for a single pay rise.

I have never been a religious person. I am not anti-religion, but neither am I a regular churchgoer. I go occasionally, Christmas time and that sort of thing, but otherwise not. I suppose I hold to Christian beliefs. And I am a very, very strong believer in the social conscience of companies. It is absolutely essential, and going to be ever more essential in the future, for companies to recognise their social responsibilities to employees, to communities, to the environment as a whole. In British Airways we were the first, or one of the very first, public companies in this country to publish an annual environmental report, which has now evolved into a full social responsibility report. That is a completely separate annual report, separate from our financial report and accounts. I cannot claim those things mattered so much to me when I was younger. I cannot recollect exactly when I became much more conscious of their importance, but I certainly have felt like that for a very long time now, both when I worked in the USA and since I have been back in Britain.

And that leads me into my concerns about the future, and about how people are going to be able to cope with the demands of their work as the business world accelerates in pace and becomes ever larger, as companies acquire, globalise and expand immensely. One of the principal factors in all of this is the speed of communication. When you are confronted by a whole stream of e-mails, with people expecting responses almost on the spot, it is of considerable concern. I myself can cheat a bit because I have my e-mails directed through my personal assistant. So she is able to monitor them, and to deal with a lot of them directly herself, without necessarily having to refer them to me. Frankly, if they all came through to me and I was handling them personally I would not get much else done. People are reluctant to write letters and memos, but do not hesitate to bang away at their keyboards with e-mails. I have a personal e-mail address but I do not give it out for business purposes. So I do not get business e-mails at weekends. Likewise mobile phones are tremendous when you need them. And they are an absolutely bloody nightmare when they ring all around you, when you are in a train or at a sports facility or wherever it might be. All this is part of the modern world and is what we have to adjust to living and working with. **99**

## Keeping Your Balance

- Telephone your partner as often as you can when travelling (and remember to have a chat with your children if they are around).

- When travelling long distances adjust immediately to the time prevalent at your destination. Switching completely to the local time is the fastest way to overcome jet-lag.

- Get important business papers distributed in time for people to read them at weekends. All managers expect to do some reading at the weekend, and it will help them cope better during the week.

# Chapter 6

# SIR GEORGE BULL

George Bull is chairman of Sainsbury's and a director of BNP Paribas UK
and the Maersk Co. Ltd. He was formerly chairman and chief executive
of International Distillers and Vintners, chairman and chief executive of
Grand Metropolitan, joint chairman of Diageo and a director of United
Business Media. A past member of the CBI President's Committee and
of the BACC Advisory Board, he is a director of the Marketing Council
and a vice-chairman of the Chartered Institute of Marketing. He is the
immediate past president of the Wine and Spirit Benevolent Society and
was president of the Advertising Association from 1996 to 2000.
George Bull was born in 1936 and educated at Ampleforth. He is
married and has four sons and one daughter.

**"**I am a guy who has just got on with the day and the week
and the year and with my life. The balance of my life and my

career has been almost 100% happenstance. It has just been how the cookie crumbled.

My wife would say, very strongly and firmly, that there has never been any question or doubt that business has always taken preference, on every occasion – and I would hotly deny this to my deathbed. But I would admit that almost invariably, if there was a clash between business and my private life, I have taken the business route and then patched matters up with the family soon afterwards. There have been exceptions of a major cataclysmic nature that have broken that rule, and it has not been a conscious rule, but when I think back I think my wife is not as far out as I have often told her she was.

I would go to great lengths to meet my children's commitments as long as I had it plotted two or three weeks or more in advance. I would slot things into the diary and make every reasonable effort then to break off business engagements and be there at the right time. On the other hand, if I had an overseas visit planned or I was at an important conference or I was doing some other such thing, then I would do those things and I am afraid not attend the school play or concert or whatever it was that was coming up.

It was not that I thought I would be putting my career at risk by missing the business event. I never much thought about the question of putting my career at risk. The motivation was much more about doing the job rather than 'Would I be risking my career by taking time off?' I just wanted to do the job as well as it could be done. I had to do what I had to do.

The companies I worked for in those days never gave such matters a thought. That was not malevolent on their part. It simply never occurred to me that they would or should think about it, any more than it occurred to me that it was not simply part of everyday life. You cut the cake the way that it lay in front of you. Those sorts of considerations did not feature.

Today they feature more than they did. By and large it is expected that people will take their full holiday entitlement. For a lot of my early life, holiday entitlements were only two weeks in the year, and I often never took the two weeks. Then it became three weeks and ultimately four weeks and for many, many years – 25 years or more – I doubt if I ever took more than half the allocated holiday I was allowed. That did not seem to me extraordinary. Absolutely nobody ever said, 'Hey, have you taken your two weeks?' It did not arise. Today people are much more conscious of the need for a balance. But not many businesses actually take time out to try to make sure that people are away from their desk as much as possible! Today the pressure in business is so great that, on the contrary, they expect people will look after themselves and take their holidays, but otherwise they keep the pressure on. There is a lot to do, everybody is overstretched. Yes, businesses are mindful of the need to make sure that people are reasonably happy and comfortable. But I do not know that it goes to the next level, pushing people out of the office and making sure they are attending school fêtes.

In the early years, particularly, I had to travel a lot. It was unavoidable. Within two or three months of getting married I went off on a ten-week tour. In those days I was an export salesman and the overseas travel was a ten-week circuit. That was quite an undertaking, just after getting married, and it sort of set the pattern. Right through my life I have spent a tremendous amount of time travelling. At one time for tax reasons we were having to log how many nights we stayed abroad. It was in the 1970s, and I was away 140 to 150 nights a year because that is what the job demanded. I got a note from British Airways the other day. I still have 2.8 million British Airways unused miles, let alone hundreds of thousands on other airlines, and those that have been used or are from airlines that have since fallen off the edge of the cliff. People said to me it must have been a terrific strain on our marriage. Well, I suppose it might have been for certain people, but for us I think it was probably a strengthener. It was so nice when I got back!

Once when I came home my third son was having supper and I had got back just in time. I had come in from a plane from the USA or somewhere and – my wife always tells this story – my son said, 'Mummy, who's that?'

My wife said, 'That's your father.'

And he replied, 'Oh Daddy, you've come home!'

My wife thinks the story is amusing, and it is, but it has always made me feel guilty. In my mind I excused it because I myself had been away to public school, and all my life I had been used to being away. But my boys went to a day-school, which was only ten miles away. That meant they were always at home in term times. So when I did come back, during holidays or terms, I was immediately back in the family with all the children. If you work it out, we were apart an awful lot less than if the children had gone to boarding-school, as I had myself. Perhaps that is just an excuse, but I did feel that in practice I was there with them a lot, and more than might have been the case had the cookie crumbled the other way. Not that my wife would have allowed them to go to boarding-school anyway – she hated it!

Working as hard and as long as I did there were moments undoubtedly when I was under stress, and I did feel at full stretch. But I did not feel resentful. I just felt, 'Wow, how am I actually going to get all this done and catch the aeroplane back to New

York on Tuesday afternoon?' or whatever. You were constantly on the move at such a speed. Yes, there was often a lot to do and you did wonder how you were going to do it. But I never felt resentful at having a lot on my plate. Most of the other people had a lot on their plates too.

I have always managed to keep up my leisure interests of varying sorts – the usual stuff. I enjoy reading. I am not great with music or plays but I have long been into photography and have a library of pictures. I have done my own developing, printing and I am now onto the computer. In the sporting area I have always played golf – not particularly well, but I have played it all my life and I touched a single-figure handicap. I played cricket when I was younger and enjoyed that, and I also shoot. So I have never been short of sporting activities. I did not do them to relax from work. I did them because I enjoyed doing them. And whichever way you look at it, the nature of my business – that is, the wine and spirit business – is vaguely linked to enjoyment. When we went to conferences there was usually a golfing contest or something. So I did get quite a lot of opportunities for relaxation when out and about on the business circuit. That provided a lot of opportunity, albeit out of a family context, for doing things that were enjoyable in their own right.

It was the same with travelling. A lot of people say, 'Whoopee, I love to travel myself – how lucky you are!' Well, I have been almost everywhere in the world and I have been very fortunate because I have enjoyed it. Then people ask: 'So where do you go on holiday?'

When we had a holiday it was usually spent in England because the last thing I wanted was to get on a plane and fly somewhere. That would have been a busman's holiday gone mad. I have had so much opportunity to go to interesting places, and meet interesting people, that if I am in a self-deprecating mood I say, 'Well, life is basically a holiday anyway. I do not need other holidays because it is so enjoyable doing what I do most of the time.' That was not so far away from the truth because I have had a wonderfully entertaining, fulfilling life with lots of things to do, lots of responsibility, lots of action, in a field of activity, which is not far removed from what most people would like to do if they were on holiday anyway.

On the other hand, my real holidays have been interrupted by business more than a few times. In the very early days it did not happen so much. My holidays were very short and probably I would not be in touch with the office. People would know where I was, so I was contactable. But that did not often arise. Gradually as seniority came, and you became more responsible, you had to keep in touch more. In the last 15 years, business interruptions have been an integral part of any holiday, and since taking on a major role as a PLC board director, my working life has constantly been on tap, with computers and with everything else. We now have a little house in France, where I am connected through to the office. When I was working full time I did at least two hours every morning while I was there. Anyway I prefer that rather than coming back to a great mailbag or to hitting a huge number of problems on arrival. It has become an integral part of my life. But that is directly relatable to seniority and responsibility.

The role of my wife has been truly amazing. She has always made just the right amount of objection. She would say, 'Look you're always working or you're away or you're off on business or you're . . .' but never to the point of putting her foot down completely, and saying, 'That's enough, you've done too much.' She has always, always made it not only possible but also easy for me to get on and do the things that she knows I have to do, while just making it tough enough to know she is still there! She has been like a picador, pricking me whenever she thought I was going too far, and has done that incredibly well. That is one of her amazingly strong attributes. Without that kind of support it would have been a lot more difficult than it was. I am eternally grateful to her for that. When I am away she gets on and does her own things, which she has always done, and that has been another huge strength.

But keeping up with the business, and travelling so much, and spending time with the family has meant I have less time than I would like for friends. I have two or three friends from school who I see occasionally, but not many, and not that often. I have a tremendous number of very friendly acquaintances rather than a clutch of real bosom pals. I have never been around doing things all the time with any friends – permanently as it were – and work has probably done that. A lot of my friendly acquaintances are related to business, but by no means all. We have lived in the same village for 30 years so we have a good coterie of friends who are not in any way related to any of the businesses I have been in.

There are occasions, cataclysmic occasions as I said before, when you just have to drop everything at business immediately. My brother had a bad stroke recently so I had to get out of the office pretty quickly and go down to Cornwall. Yes, there are specific instances where one has simply turned around and gone back to base helter-skelter. Although I always say business comes first, there are times when I have come back on an earlier flight or whatever is necessary to get to some vital event. But not many. It takes something pretty cataclysmic to cause me to deviate off course.

I am far from proud of it, but I have gone abroad occasionally even when my wife has been really quite ill. I go. She does not expect me not to go. But when she had a most monumental accident while we were at a conference in California, I was on business and there was a stack of things that needed to be done and I just had to stop immediately. I stayed with her for three solid weeks. The support my then boss gave me was fantastic. He said, 'I will take over and do all your work.' Everybody else in Grand Met rallied and helped and they were fantastic too. That was the worst possible occasion. I was away, I was on business, and I had to stop and get off the roundabout there and then. I worked in Minneapolis thereafter for three months because my wife had to stay in hospital in Minneapolis. I made the adjustments that were necessary. I literally had to alter my life immediately. But fortunately the children had all grown up and left home by then, so there was nobody dependent on us at that point. And it just so happened I was lucky because I could operate out of Minneapolis as easily as I could out of London. Still, it was a tough time. Much tougher for my wife, of course, than for me.

I occasionally look back and run over things in my mind – 'Was I fair? Have I been right?' – and the answer is: I do not know. Yes, I do have momentary twinges of guilt about not being present enough at home, either for not quite enough time or not at enough special events. There are all sorts of things where I am definitely guilty as charged, and to say I am not or that I have never thought about it would be untrue. I have missed things and I have felt guilty. But against that I feel that I did what I had to do. When people ask, 'Did you plan your life?' the answer of course is 'No'. I find it astonishing when people say, 'Oh well, I will do two and a half years here as a stepping-stone' and so on. I have never liked employing anybody in a business I was running who was using me as a stepping-stone to something else. Maybe I am very old-fashioned, but when you went into a job you did it hell for leather as well as you could, with whatever limitations you might have. If you did it well enough, the chances are something else would pop out of the woodwork, and they would say, 'Oh well, you know, let's have him, he might be able to . . .' By doing each job as well as you could, you eventually moved along. Each time I got another promotion the most astonished person in the world was me. And then there was nothing else for it but do the new job as well as you could, and so you went on. But at the end of it you could return to the family with some benefits that accrued out of working as hard as you had to in the earlier times. So I think as the wheel has gone round the balance probably is not so far out of equilibrium. I do not have sleepless nights worrying about it, but I would simply be telling a lie if I said that it has never crossed my mind.

Looking at my life, rightly or wrongly, I have achieved a certain amount – I would not want to exaggerate this, but I have achieved some things – and not too much at other people's expense. I have been very lucky. On the other hand I am an absolutely fundamental believer that the end does not justify the means. It happens that the end result was where I have ended up, and maybe I would not have ended up here if I had not done all those things. When the wheel has finally turned right round, things have balanced out.

There is another thing. Both my wife and myself have always been practising Catholics and this brings us a kind of peace, insofar as anybody can find peace in life. Do I sit down and quickly read the Bible, a chapter a day? 'No' is the answer. But there is a constant sense of being, which is there all the time; and wherever I have been in the world – absolutely wherever – the number of times I have missed going to Mass on a Sunday is countable practically on the fingers of one hand. You have this discipline that wherever you are travelling you will still find where you can get to Mass. It is a question of discipline, and of holding onto the yard-arm a bit. It gives you a perspective. And it never quite goes away. It is a sheet-anchor.

I have never done this kind of analysis before in such depth, ever. I often think I ought to have done things so much better and planned so much better, but my life did not happen that way. Anyway things have worked out I think. They have worked out pretty well, really. **99**

## Keeping Your Balance

- Analyse your own work/life balance from time to time. Try not to view it either too harshly or through rose-tinted spectacles. If it seems wrong, change things. Whether you like it or not, you will end up reviewing the balance you achieved, and by then it will be too late to make amends.

- Choose leisure interests that can be integrated with work – photography is ideal if you travel a lot. Balancing your work and your life is not simply about spending time with your family; it is about achieving a healthy mental balance in your own life.

- The same is true of religion. If you have strong religious convictions do not let work impede them.

# Chapter 7

# SIR CHRISTOPHER BLAND

Christopher Bland is chairman of BT. Formerly he was chairman of the BBC Board of Governors, of LWT Holdings, of the Century Hutchinson Group, of NFC, of Life Sciences International and of Sir Joseph Cawston. He was deputy chairman of the Independent Broadcasting Authority and a director of the National Provident Institution and of Storehouse. He has also been chairman of the Hammersmith Hospitals NHS Trust. Christopher Bland was born in 1938 and educated at Sedbergh School and the Queen's College, Oxford. He is married and has a son, two stepsons and two stepdaughters.

**"E**very reaction has an equal and opposite reaction. In the Thatcherite 1980s a lot of people in some sectors of business and industry went too far in terms of allowing their work to dominate their lives. Now there has been a swing in the opposite direction. People are talking more about the existence of a concept that 20 years ago was not much discussed. That is a positive move forward if you are – as I am – someone who believes work and personal life have got to be kept in balance. There is also at least anecdotal evidence that in America, post-11 September 2001, people are thinking, 'If life is as dangerous and as difficult as that event makes it seem, perhaps it is not a great idea to spend all my time with my nose up against the grindstone.'

In the early 1960s employers did not think about the subject. When they hired you they thought they had bought you, and that is how they expected you to behave. Even then there were a few enlightened exceptions. Corporations like Shell probably were enlightened then, but there were not many of them. Nobody ever mentioned 'work/life balance' to me in my first 20 years in business. In my early days I would occasionally have to tell tales to get time off – grandmother's funeral's on the day of the university rugby match, that kind of thing. But I did not do it often. Had I done so my employers would have seen through it straight away.

Today the Human Resources people talk about work/life balance in a way that they didn't even ten years ago. They had not even heard of it then. It probably had not been invented as a phrase then, and it would be interesting to know when it first started to be talked about widely. I would guess ten years ago would be about right. But now it is a pretty important factor, very important for example in the BBC, where Greg Dyke is a leader in personally encouraging people to have a proper work/life balance – and he certainly does so himself.

The problems are obviously tougher for working women with families, but nowadays good employers do try to take some of the strain out of it. For example, job-sharing is now quite common.

When I first started in business it had not been heard of. Now job-sharing occurs in all big organisations and that is particularly beneficial to women, as is maternity leave, and even paternity leave. Homeworking is now actively encouraged and technology, particularly our technology at BT, makes that really quite easy and effective to arrange. So all those add up to quite a change.

But in the end you have to plan to achieve your own balance. It will not occur by happenstance. You learn how to do it for yourself. Nobody really teaches you. Obviously it is much easier to plan when you are the boss than when you are not, and there have been occasions in my life – after all, most of my life I have not been the boss – when I worked very hard indeed in terms of hours and travel. But I was single, I was young, and I enjoyed it. I had a horrible 12 months in a bank in the City where I was not the boss, where I had to work very hard, and where I did not enjoy the job at all. That was a bad experience. The imbalance was not under my control and I could not do much about it. Since then I have learned to control my work/life balance pretty well.

To my mind, the mechanisms revolve around three things – first, working hours during the week and how you manage those; allied to that, how much business entertaining you either want or have to do. Second weekends, and third holidays.

When I started in business we worked Saturday mornings. So I myself go back to the five-and-a-half-day week. Today I am an 'eight-thirty to six' man pretty religiously. I work after six when I have to, but not very often. I will have a breakfast meeting at seven-thirty if I have to, but not very often. And I avoid business lunches like the plague, so my eight-thirty to six is not interrupted by a two-hour break in the middle where I have to go off and waste time over food that I do not need. I probably entertain less than I should, certainly not more than once or twice a month. In some businesses that would be too little. I am fortunate to have avoided the excessive entertaining that is demanded in, say, the banking business or the advertising business. So that is the first thing – controlling working hours during the week.

Next, what about the weekends? I am pretty careful about weekends. I hardly ever do any work at weekends. I do not take work home. If I cannot do it during the week it waits until Monday. There are exceptions, but not many. I do not telephone people at the weekends unless I really have to, and I expect them to treat me in the same way. If they have to telephone me, and sometimes they do, that is fine, but if it is something that could have waited until Monday or that they should have dealt with on Friday, then they should not have to 'phone me, and I would tell them so. Nobody sends me business e-mails at home. They have occasionally sent me e-mails on holiday when that has been the best means of communication, but last weekend I did not look at my computer at all. So it is no e-mails. People occasionally send me a fax at the weekend, if something is really important.

I had to do half a day's work this weekend but that is pretty rare. If you make a point of taking work home at the weekends then you are working a six- or seven-day week and that does not work for me. Working that way is not very effective, certainly not in my own case. There is no correlation between the number of hours I work and the effectiveness of my performance. If anything there is an inverse correlation after about an eight- or nine-hour day and a five-day week. I would be worse if I worked 12 hours a day, six days a week. The performance curve would drop radically. So you have got to manage the weekends, and I do.

Finally holidays. When I started out I was allowed only two

weeks, then three or four, and now I take five or six weeks' holiday a year. I am absolutely unabashed about it. I have always taken the maximum allowed, and I have never thought there is any virtue in those people who say, 'I haven't had a holiday for three years.' That is shocking. It is bad management on their part and bad management on their superior's part. I have taken phone calls and received faxes on holiday, but never cut a holiday short. I have cancelled an occasional long weekend, if I have had to. I was due to be away Thursday and Friday this week as it happens, and now I can't. It turned out to be just bad timing. And that is fair enough, as I was eating into the working week. I was going to have a three-day week, and life is too complicated at the moment.

Mobiles, e-mails and faxes do make business life much easier. They make working from home easier, if you want to work from home. They make going on trips, on journeys, much easier. You can go on a five- or six-hour train journey and keep in touch so you do not lose a whole day. But it also means that unless you turn your mobile off – and they do turn off – you can be got at wherever you are, more or less.

Though I am quite robust, if the hours pile up I do not think as clearly, and I get tired, and I get bored. And none of those is an ideal background to the making of good decisions, or of helping other people to make them. Every now and again I feel pissed off or enraged or disappointed. But I do not feel I need a tranquilliser or to go and lie down in a room for a day. And I do not dream about work – or only very rarely. I can count on the fingers of one hand the sleepless nights I have had over business.

Since becoming a chairman I have certainly set a clear example. If others have chosen not to follow it then I probably have not done a lot to stop them. But I have made it very clear that if people boast about the holidays they have not taken, I am unimpressed by such boasts. Here at BT we have a good HR operation that pays attention to people's work/life balance. Most big corporations now take it as a matter of course that they should look after such things. It is enlightened self-interest. If people work more effectively the company will benefit. People stay with the company longer and do not burn out. There are some businesses – corporate finance; any kind of trading, be it stock market or options or futures or pork bellies; management consulting; perhaps the advertising business from time to time – those types of business are particularly demanding in terms of hours. They are personal service businesses with pretty rigid and inescapable deadlines. And if they charge their clients on the basis of an eight-hour day but get 12 to 16 hours out of their staff, that is good for profitability. At least in the short term. But in a normal corporation none of that is necessary. It is counterproductive.

Organising my work/life balance has been easier for me because I got married and had children late. I was 45 when my son was born and I was already a boss then. I was chairman of the company. The great thing about being chairman is that you control other people's diaries. Rather than have them say, 'You have got to be here on a certain date' you can move stuff around or arrange stuff in advance. So I have been a good school speech day and sports match attender. I cannot think of an occasion when I did not attend a family or school event because of a business meeting, however important. I used to avoid my son's prep school speech days like the plague but that was because they were the most unbearably tedious occasions and I would do anything to duck them. That was deliberate, so I certainly never felt bad about it.

And since I have had a family I have not had jobs that demanded much travelling. Not by the standards of international business-men, anyway. I travelled quite a lot when I was single. That was different. Getting sent to live in Rome for four months did not exactly play hell with my personal life. Indeed I can vividly remember it enhancing it. It was not exactly a punishment posting.

I have become increasingly aware that it is important to control your diary and give yourself time to think. I do not mean on top of a peak in the north-west of Scotland, but thinking in the office. If you do not control the diary in organisations like the BBC and BT – both very greedy for time – they can clutter your mind and your life with ambassadorial functions that are not that valuable. You have got to do some of them, but you never have to do as many as the invitations that you get. If you accept all of those – go to every foreign state's national day, for example, or every embassy dinner or every leaving party or every seminar for equal opportunities – then you shouldn't. You have to do some of it, but you do not have to accept every invitation to lunch or dinner or a seminar or a conference. I am quite gregarious. I enjoy a conference in Aspen, Colorado, or Sun Valley, Idaho, as well as the next man but I am also reasonably realistic, about the time it takes and about the value that it gives to the company, and to me.

Corporations should not get involved with people's personal lives in a judgmental way, but they have to be aware of what is happening in individual employees' lives and make allowances for them. Maybe I have been lucky but there have hardly ever been family crises that have required a business cancellation. I remember when my father had his first coronary. I dropped everything and went straight to the hospital. But everybody understands that kind of crisis. There are other crises that might be less dramatic but equally compelling – such as problems with children, which crop up from time to time – that people would not have understood in the past, or anyway not accepted as being a justification for dropping everything. Today I would expect our HR people to know if somebody's wife had leukaemia, say – or somebody's husband come to that – and if the employee concerned was having a hard time as a result I would expect us to make allowances and indeed to help in whatever way we could. Or if someone was on the verge of a divorce they could talk to the HR people. That would be up to them. There are some people who would rather keep quiet about things like that, and that is an individual's personal decision. Some may simply prefer to get through things like that on their own. If they do go to talk to the HR department that reflects well on the HR department, because it means they must think they will get a receptive hearing.

Of course any welfare issue can be a licence for scroungers or slackers, but in the end the genuine slacker will be discovered. And it will not be because they are taking all their holiday entitlement every year. It will be because while they are at work they are not doing a very good job.

My friends are very important to me. It is one of the things in life that gives me greatest pleasure, so we see a lot of our friends. We nearly always go on holiday with friends. We have friends to stay with us in the country pretty regularly. We meet them in London. What is my preferred idea of a good night out? It is going to the theatre and having dinner with a couple of people who I am really fond of. The two sources of my longstanding friends are university – people I met at Oxford – and people I met through the Bow Group – people like Leon Brittan, Norman Lamont and Michael Howard; they are all still my friends. Not many of my close friends come from business – although I suppose politics was a kind of business for me then.

I am proud of being a businessman. If we do things right and do them properly we make a positive contribution to society and to the world. And if not, not! I have no guilt about being a businessman – quite the reverse. And I do not feel guilty, on the whole, about my work/life balance over the years. Most people, unless they are battered by life and by circumstances, do what they want to do. People who work six days a week, 12 hours a day – why do they do that? They do it because they want to. They might be working for a particularly demanding merchant bank or corporate lawyer, but they will be paid half-a-million quid a year for doing that at the age of 35, and that is what they want to do. They do not have to. They could do something else.

You probably could not prove it but I think there is a correlation between a good work/life balance and your mental and physical health, and if in turn you are mentally and physically in reasonable shape then you will live longer, be happier and probably do better work. You may not be able to prove it, but you cannot prove everything that we know in our hearts to be true. People who are burned out, exhausted, nervous, frightened, do not really do very good stuff in the long run. So there is an important health issue here, and that is at the core of why it is you have to take work/life balance seriously. **"**

## Keeping Your Balance

- Evaluate your most productive personal work schedule; working stressfully long hours over the long haul is a lose-lose-lose situation. If you burn yourself out your family, your career and your health will all suffer.

- The more often you work through lunch, the less often you will need to work late or take work home.
- Be picky about out-of-hours business invitations. Most people accept far more than they need to.

# Chapter 8

---

# ROSALYN WILTON

Rosalyn Wilton is chief executive of Hemscott. She was formerly a
director of GNI, managing director of Drexel Burnham Lambert, a
director of LIFFE and of Reuters Transaction Products, a member
of Reuters Executive Committee and a non-executive director
of Scottish Widows.
Rosalyn Wilton was born in 1952 and educated at London University.
She is married and has two daughters.

**"F**or a mother, things are easier today than they would have
been 20 years ago because of the number of support services available, such as crèches, the availability of additional nursery
care, Internet shopping and, above all, the acceptance of women
in business. Twenty-five years ago or so I had to leave work to
have my children. I went back two and a half years later because I

felt I wanted to work, and then had to balance both working life and motherhood at the same time.

I never really thought of myself as having a problem, or even difficulties. Both myself and my husband share the responsibility for our children together, and if one of our children was not well and needed one of us, then it would be whichever one of us that was available more instantly or more easily at that point in time. And in the event that something was a problem, we were extremely fortunate in that we employed help at home for the children. Both our sets of parents live far away and were not able to help us, so even if the helpers were just sitting there waiting for the school to phone up to say, 'Your daughter is sick. We need someone to collect her' that was a huge reassurance. It is something I always felt prepared to pay for, and I would have found it very difficult to work had I not always had that at the back of my mind, to allay my worries.

I firmly believe that if you want something enough you make it happen. My husband and I were in good positions, and we worked very, very hard. We left home extremely early in the morning to work in the City and came back late. It was tough, and even finding someone to be at home covering all those hours was difficult. We left at around a quarter to seven in the morning and got back over 12 hours later, at around half-past seven at night. But I do not believe anything is impossible and there are plenty of women who work – and we have women working here at Hemscott – who have children and are balancing their home life with their working life, and they enjoy the interaction with people in the office and would miss that if they sat at home the whole time. They do not all have help at home by any means. It is entirely dependent on the individual, and one must allow individuals to make their own decisions.

Retrospectively it is easy to say I planned my home life and working life. But I am not sure that at the time I sat down and said, 'I have to balance this out.' When I left work initially to have my children, I felt that I would be giving up work completely, that I had retired. I was in my twenties and I found shortly after that – within months – that I missed the intellectual interaction, the intellectual challenge of work, and I felt I had to get back to work. I have always felt a need to do something. Having had my two children and not gone back to work in-between, I then went back into work full time, and I love both working and having a family. At the end of the day – if, God forbid, there was any crisis – the children would always come first. Always. But I would expect that of any working father, too.

And fortunately for me there has been nothing tragic. One daughter had to go into hospital with suspected appendicitis, for example, and I dealt with it immediately. My personal assistants at work have always known that if either the nanny or one of my daughters phoned up and said, 'I need to speak to . . .' that would mean it is urgent. I would expect the PA to interrupt me, wherever I was. But on the other side, my children and my nanny, when they want to speak to me, will also phone up and say, 'It's not urgent.' They know the difference between urgent matters and when they just want to speak to me. We all respect that division.

I could not be successful in business if I did not have a very happy and settled family life, which is my rock. If I were going home every night to a family in turmoil or disagreement, I could never concentrate on my job and I would be very unsuccessful. So it is the combination of the two that has worked so well for me. But it might be different for other people. And I had to learn to cope as I went along, as things came. I started in the City in 1973 when there were very few women and I do not know if there were any working mums at all. It was not anything that there was any precedent for. So I did what came naturally to me.

I have always taken work home. I have always carried work in my bag going home and at the weekends. On holiday I have always been available at the end of a line, if there was a critical issue that had to have a decision and I was the only one that could make that decision. Anyway I like to keep in touch. I have never had to come back from holiday, but I have certainly been tracked down on various beaches in remote places.

And I had to travel a lot. I commuted to New York for over a year, going almost every other week, and I travelled very extensively around the world running businesses in a lot of different countries, on my own, without the family. It was not easy but I tried to organise it to coincide with my children's needs. The craziest thing I did was to fly back from Australia to go to a parents' evening. I flew back straight from Australia and got picked up at Heathrow and went straight to my daughter's parents' evening because I knew it would be devastating if all her friends had both parents present and her mother was not there. I have always made a point of coming back at weekends, from wherever I am – whether it is Singapore or Australia. So it has been quite crazy, but it has happened. I tried to do less travelling during school holidays, but during the summer there is less business travel anyway, because other people are on holiday too. So that worked out pragmatically.

On one of my many trips to New York there was a particular girlfriend who worked about 18 hours a day, like me, while we were there, and when we discussed this she said, 'Oh, I have to keep working because I feel so guilty being away from home.' I remember being in Tokyo and being taken to a sumo match and I thought, 'I'm enjoying myself. I'm on business. I should not be socialising.' When you get back from a business trip people ask, 'Did you go sightseeing?' I have never, never gone sightseeing on a single business trip. I have only gone sightseeing with my husband and my children and I would feel hugely guilty if there was any element of pleasure or enjoyment, other than business enjoyment, on any business trip. Apparently I am not the only one who thinks that. My girlfriend was exactly the same. But I have never heard a man say that. Men go and do all sorts of things on business trips! As a woman you almost feel you have to justify your trip away from home, by just about killing yourself by working all times of the day and night. It is extraordinary. You do feel guilty. You try to cram in as much as possible and not give yourself a moment off.

We have a small set of close friends. We have some very close friends who appreciate the fact that I work and my husband worked. But that is quite difficult for some people to understand. In business you get invited to a lot of different functions and, because we really treasure our family time together at weekends, I resent other people – even friends – interfering with that. And though our friends are business people they are not generally people we have worked with. Maybe one or two, but more come from outside of our work. I can count on one hand the number of friends – real friends that I can call sincere friends – that I have met in business. There are people you have worked with over time, but when you really need a friend there are very few of those, and I think that goes for almost everyone. Someone who worked with me once said, 'You don't work in the City to get friends.' He added 'If you want a friend, buy yourself a dog!'

I absolutely could not do this job unless my husband fully supported me, fully respected me for what I do. That has been the

single most important component in me being able to do all my
jobs. He was also in the City so we understand each other's
businesses and are able to talk about them if necessary, just to
relieve ourselves of some of the frustrations of the daily routine.
And if there are major issues brewing he will know because I most
probably will not be in the best frame of mind, or in the best
mood.

Sometimes I mull things over without speaking. Most of the
time I put problems into my head and then wait for the answers to
come. I will strategise in my own mind and come out with the
answers and conclusions. But it is very useful to have another set
of trusting ears, ears that understand your business as well as
being understanding to you as an individual, and knowing how
you react to things on a personal basis. And both my parents – my
father is 91 and my mother is 87 – give me business advice to this
very day!

But having elderly parents brings its own problems. I was once
about to present to a very large room chock full of high-powered
analysts in New York, and I had been told 15 minutes beforehand
that my mother had suffered a severe heart attack. What could I
do? She was in hospital. I do not know how I did it but I went
straight onto the stage and made a presentation and carried on
perfectly normally and after that, without stopping, I went straight
to the airport and jumped on a plane. I remember thinking to
myself at the time, 'There is no point in panicking, there is no
point me getting worried. I cannot do anything – she is in the best
place. There is nothing I can physically do. The extra minutes will
not make any difference.' I was thinking that during the presentation and it was very, very tough. That was probably one of my
toughest times in business, when I had to put on a brave face.

Fortunately she got through it and she is fine. But I could not be sure of that at the time. I was told on the phone that her heart attack was very, very serious.

As a working mother myself, having been through it, if my PA, who has two young children, wanted to collect her daughter from some event or go to a parents' evening and wanted to leave early – then the children are a priority and that should be the same for her as for me. And if I were to say 'No, you can't go', how happy would she be working in that sort of company? We all have to accept that if you have children they are the highest priority. Nobody wants to feel they are working in a company that does not appreciate that. Some women who feel very guilty about taking off time because their children are ill, or they have to go to the school or something, will phone up and say, 'The dishwasher's leaked and I have to wait. It's all flooded and I have to wait for the electrician to come round, or the plumber.' They think that will be perfectly acceptable, but would never say, 'Well, actually my daughter's ill and I've got to stay at home.' That kind of lying happens a lot. It is a common phenomenon that women feel guilty if they take off time because their child is ill, but do not feel guilty if they have to wait for the electrician, because that is a more accepted thing. Everyone knows electricians never turn up on time. I have always been straight. I have two children – you either accept it or you do not. And I do not like positive discrimination. I would hate to think that I got into senior positions because I was a woman. I would not have lasted long if I were promoted for the wrong reasons. It would have shone out very quickly.

Things are easier for men because most of their wives are at home, or a lot of them are. Having said that, there are now a lot more women who are working or doing part-time work. It should not be any more difficult or easy for men, but the fact is that there are still more working men than working women, so most men have women at home to look after things. Not that all women want to go out to work. There are plenty of women who just do not want to go that extra mile. It might be to do with the children. Or they might just feel that they do not want to be out there. My very best friend does not work and has not worked since she has had children and I respect her for it.

E-mails and mobiles make it easier to communicate for women, particularly for women who cannot go out to work for one reason or another, maybe they have a permanently sick child at home but want to do things. They can do more things at home now with technology, and with the Internet. So I think new technology has been a huge plus in general. Modern technology need not be intrusive. It is the individual's decision.

Nor do I expect those who work for me to be available on a 24/7 basis. But I can be pretty demanding. I expect people to be passionate about their job, to believe in what they do, and to do it as a 100% commitment. Does that mean they need to be on 24/7? The answer is no. Nobody needs to be on 24/7, including myself. There are times when we might need to work outside of the office on a Sunday, as that may be the only time we can meet. Fortunately for me the executive directors of this company have the same view – we want to be winners and to be winners you have to do more than other people. A year ago we were on the phone to each other every Sunday, Boxing Day, Christmas Day, New Year's Day, New Year's Eve – all the time – because there was so much going on. There is less need for it now and if someone called me they would be calling me not to waste my time, but because they felt it was important to contact me. It is as simple as that.

In my previous jobs I used to get faxes constantly. I would get phone calls in the middle of the night. When I was at Reuters I would have phone calls at three o'clock in the morning. I was not over the moon about it. My husband was even less over the moon than I was because I am better at getting back to sleep than he is. But I do not generally expect people to be interrupted in their private lives. It is putting the hours in during the day and making sure you feel passionate about your business that is important.

Now I am running a UK-based company, without the travel, it is certainly less stressful. There are no two ways about it. Flying the number of miles I did, being away every other week in one particular year, then several times a year to Asia and around the world to Eastern Europe, back to Australia, back over here, is unquestionably pressurising. I loved it at the time. It was great fun and it achieved results. Had it not achieved results it would have been very, very stressful. But because there were positive results it was extremely satisfying. You are working 18 hours a day, and you still feel guilty about the number of times you are away from home, especially if there is an issue that should keep you at home – not something tragic, just a small issue that you would want to be at home for. I remember that after my year of commuting I took the whole family on a big surprise holiday to the American West Coast and did all the lovely sightseeing things because I felt so guilty about having been away so much. I booked this wonderful holiday, did not tell them where they were going, other than the States. It happened twice actually, and that was the result of pure guilt.

I have not really got other hobbies apart from going to the gym or doing aerobics. I have always had a passion for business, even as a child. So I always say my hobby is my business. I do not get stressed by the pressure of both being at home and being in the office. The converse is true. I enjoy the differences between being in a very fast-moving job and then going back to my family with different values. I love those extremes. I spend the weekends doing things with the children, and that occupies just about all the time, and it can be very tiring too! There have been times on a Sunday night when I think, 'I can't wait to go back to work for a rest.' I am interested in antiques so I wander round antique shops, but I am not a great hobbyist at all.

I have always been ambitious, and competitive, but I am certainly not competitive in sport because I am no good at it. I know where to compete and where not. Would I be ambitious to the detriment of my family life? I would still be ambitious but I would be hugely unsuccessful and terribly unhappy. I like the challenge of business. I like to do things against the odds – to knock down a few barriers. It is great selling to someone who says they absolutely will not do any business with you. As soon as someone says that I come up thinking, 'Oh yes, you will.' I like tangible results. I like moving the goalposts forward the whole time. I think that is what keeps me motivated. It is nice to earn money as well but I could not just do it for the money if I were not happy about all those other things.

I do not know whether religion has helped me. Everyone knows I am Jewish, everyone knows I am a mother, everyone knows I have a husband, everyone knows I have daughters and I never hide any of that. One of the mistakes some women make is they think: oh gosh, if they have got a child then they cannot get a job. But my girls came up into the dealing rooms I worked in when they were young children, they used to come to the office at Reuters, and they come up here at Hemscott and I talk about work to them because I am interested to hear their views – out of the mouths of babes and so on. But has religion played a part? Maybe in the way I have been brought up, and in family values, the way I approach family life. Nothing more than that.

I am not really a 'look-back' person. I think it is my trading instinct. You cannot survive on yesterday's trades, you have to look to tomorrow's. So I have never looked back and said, 'That should have been different.' I did what I did, and fortunately for me it worked out well. Would I have done anything different? I do not know if I would. I do not know what the 'different' would have been. Would I have done less travel? Well, it was up to me – or to some extent it was. I was asked to relocate to the States by my company and I did not do so because first, my husband had a senior position, and second my daughters were very happy at their school and with their friends, and I did not want to disrupt those family roots. That is why I ended up commuting to America. The company knew that would be my answer. But they would have preferred me to relocate.

As I said at the outset, I am firmly of the belief that if you want something enough then you can make it happen. If people say, 'I can't do something', I think 'can't' is not the right word. They do not want to do it. Women *can* balance family life with working life. Lots now do. But equally I have complete respect for women who want to stay at home and be housewives, if that is their decision. **"**


## Keeping Your Balance

- Whatever the company's rules, make clear to anyone who reports to you personally that you respect their need to achieve a proper work/life balance, and you will always be sympathetic to their personal needs.

- Bring your children to your workplace now and again, explain to them what you do, introduce them to everyone – and before you know where you are their advice will be well be worth listening to!
- Let your PA know that if your children call you will speak to them immediately, whatever you are doing – and let your children know they should not insist on interrupting you unless it is really urgent.
- When you have been travelling endlessly, or been working endless hours for endless weeks, redress the balance with a family 'treat' – an unscheduled holiday, or at least a long weekend away.

# Chapter 9

## SIR PETER DAVIS

Peter Davis is group chief executive of Sainsbury's. Formerly he has been group chief executive of Prudential, chief executive and then chairman of Reed International and chairman of Reed Elsevier. He is a member of the Policy Commission on the Future of Farming and Food, a director of UBS in Switzerland, and has been a director of Boots, Cadbury Schweppes, Granada and BSB. He has been chairman of Business in the Community, of the Welfare to Work New Deal Task Force, of the Basic Skills Agency and of the National Advisory Council for Education and Training Targets. He is a trustee of the Royal Opera House, chairman of the Royal Opera House foundation, and was a founder director of the Marketing Council.

Peter Davis was born in 1941 and educated at Shrewsbury School. He is married with two sons and one daughter.

**"T**he question of work/life balance is now firmly on the agenda. People are thinking about it and talking about it, and that in itself is good. We are now in its second phase. In the early days it was about how women could cope, juggling jobs and families. It has now gone into a second phase, which concerns men as well as women – though the pressures are clearly greater for those women who are breadwinners, who have serious demanding jobs and are trying to run a family.

I have been lucky in that my wife is quite firm about these things. She has always tried to make sure that when I get home I leave the office at the office. For years she banned me opening my briefcase at weekends and, with her encouragement and coaching, I have tried to compartmentalise my work and home lives. For years I used to commute back home every night so that I would see the family, and it is only in the last eight or nine years that I have started to stay in London increasingly during the week. The pressure builds up on business dinners – and I have taken on outside responsibilities, and that adds to the overall pressure too. So now the deal we have is that, provided I leave weekends free, my wife accepts that I am going to be pretty busy during the week. I try to keep weekends clear so that we can do things together and do family things. She comes into town once or twice during the week if we are doing something together or there is a function she is coming to. Otherwise – now that the children have left home – she gets on with her things in the week and I get on with my business life. It is dependent on her having her own interests and being prepared to do things on her own. I know of other wives who find that very difficult because they do not have their own interests.

And I try to make sure that I talk to the children during the week. I have a rule that if one of the children phones I come out of meetings immediately to talk to them. They do not phone me at work unless there is something important. Otherwise they will phone in the evening or on the mobile. If they phone at work it is because of something important to them, and they do not abuse it so that is fine.

On the average day I leave the house at seven-fifteen and I will have done a good hour's work before that. If I am not out at something the night before I might do two or three hours that evening and not get up so early. But one way or another, overnight there will certainly be two or three hours' homework – what ministers would call 'in their boxes' – as well as whatever function I have to attend. This week I have a dinner or function each night – Monday, Tuesday, Wednesday and Thursday – so it will mean working when I get home from the dinner and again in the morning before I leave for work. At weekends I do family stuff – paying bills, organising pensions and investments, whatever else it may be – the necessary paperwork. But that is personal and most weekends I can get away with not doing any business work. I am on-line but I do not connect to the office over the weekend because I am not a natural e-mailer. I do use it, but not as heavily as some of my younger colleagues.

We spend our summer holiday in North Wales, and I have done for 57 years, in the same spot on Anglesey, so I am then only a train journey away. I have come back for a day in the middle of a holiday a number of times. I do not like doing it but sometimes it is necessary. I feel very strongly about taking my holiday entitlement. It was more difficult earlier in my career, but for the last five years I have taken my full holiday entitlement. I have never returned from a holiday abroad. I cannot think of a holiday abroad that has been interrupted that way. I can think of holidays abroad that have been interrupted by a lot of telephone calls, but if you have been doing the sort of job that I have done for the last three jobs, which have involved either recovery or strategic redirection – at Reed, the Pru, and here at Sainsbury's – you cannot do all that without being constantly available. Inevitably the chief executive needs to be there, at the end of a telephone.

You are ultimately responsible and have to be ultimately contactable if there is an emergency. We had a big security scare here recently and I was on a bus in the north-east Dales, with the Food and Farming Commission, but because my colleagues were all out visiting stores that day, or at suppliers, or at their children's half-term in a couple of cases, I was the most senior person that could be reached. So I had to deal with it from a bus in the north-east Dales. That was fine. But when you add that kind of thing on top of unreasonable hours for too long, the combination can get you down. It can get anyone down. Perhaps the most visible sign of stress is tetchiness. So regular holidays are an important recharging of batteries. Weekends are an important recharge of the batteries, too. Nonetheless it can be stressful. I am lucky in that I sleep pretty well. I am unfit but reasonably healthy. And I am pretty resilient. I always bounce back.

In the days the children were at school I do not think I missed a teacher/parent evening. My wife would carefully schedule them late in the evening if she could, so she was not pushing her luck! I made a particular effort to be at sports days too. That took precedence over business. Now I am a governor of the school that all my three children went to at one point, although I am not as regular an attender at governors' meetings as I would like to be these days.

Fitting in travelling can be very difficult. If you are at the top of an organisation it is easier because you have some influence over when you travel or when company functions are held, and if you are ahead of the game and are careful you can mould the company's agenda to your own – a bit, at least. To that extent it is easier once you are one of the people setting the pace. But anyway the job I did most travelling in was at the Pru, and by the time I got to the Pru the children had left school, or were on the tail end of school, so it was not a big issue. I could usually juggle things.

You were much more conscious of the difficulties of balancing your private and business lives 15 or 20 years ago. If you took time off you would either try to not make it obvious, or you would try and make up for it in other ways. The company would only be understanding if you took a day's holiday, or half a day off as holiday. Going back a bit, I have seen people invent opportunities to be somewhere out of the office so that it was less obvious they were with their children. You were much more conscious of the guilt trip of doing it then. But the need for such deception is far less necessary now. People are far more relaxed about it. As an employer, if someone says, 'I've got to leave at four because it is the parent's evening at school' as long as they have given some advance notice there is no debate. At the Pru I introduced paternity leave before it was legally required. If someone's wife was having a baby and he wanted time off, you would always give it anyway. So it was not a big thing as far as I was concerned.

If you have a lot of women going on maternity leave or a lot of people taking a lot of time off for family reasons, inevitably that puts more pressure on their colleagues. Provided everyone accepts that we all go through different stages over time, then the thing evens itself out in a big organisation – but in a small department it can be an enormous pressure. I am sympathetic with people who say, 'We are only a small department and we've lost X or Y again for such-and-such a reason.' That has to be sorted. And none of us like people who swing the lead or do not pull their weight. That is not acceptable. Some people do not want to bring their personal issues into their worklife. That is understandable, but then it is their choice. Still, generally people prefer to work for an employer who is sympathetic to these issues.

If you are in a high-profile job at a high-profile retailer like Sainsbury's, you never quite get away from work. I remember getting a postcard from a very old friend when I came back to Sainsbury's saying, 'You fool. It has taken 15 years for people to stop talking to you at dinner parties about Sainsbury's and now you've walked straight back into it.' Women all have good or bad stories and they do like to tell you them. They like to tell the bad stories more than the good, naturally. A couple of times in the last six months I have had to say to someone after about three-quarters of an hour of this, 'Actually I'm here to enjoy myself, not to have a business discussion!' It is a risk in the business I am in, but it is quite a nice risk. You know it means Sainsbury's is important to them. So wherever you are going it is not always possible to know that you will not find yourself discussing business that night.

I do not generally discuss business problems with my wife. She is not one of those wives who, when you get home, says, 'What did you do at the office today?' and wants to hear the gossip. She is not interested in who said what to whom and whether it has been a good month or a bad month or whether sales are up this week. But she is interested when we are bringing out the results, and in knowing if they are good or bad, as her friends phone her up and say, 'Did you see Sainsbury's . . .?'

She has a shrewd understanding of the business and she has been a very useful person to bounce career decisions off, because she has an intuitive judgment of people. On one occasion she said, 'You should not do business with that man' and she was right. I did, and it was a mistake and I seriously regretted it. When I decided, 15 years ago, that I had had enough of Sainsbury's I talked to her one night when I was really frustrated, and I remember her saying, 'The best thing you ever did was join Sainsbury's, but the best thing you can do now is to leave it because you are not happy.' When I told her I had been approached to go back, she said, 'Well, it's very simple. Someone needs to sort them out. So if you want to do it you may as well do it.'

I became a member of Lloyds years ago and I explained to her why I wanted to do so – the accountant said it was a good idea and all the rest of it – and she said, 'I am really worried about the house. I do not want the house put on the line.'

'That's fine,' I said. We didn't put the house on the line. We structured things so that it was not necessary. But about nine months later she was not sleeping well.

'What's the matter?' I asked.

And she said, 'I am still really worried about Lloyds.'

That was long before all the bad publicity. I asked, 'Why?'

'You get all this paper from them and you don't read it and I don't think you understand it. I think you have joined Lloyds because it is the smart thing to do, not because you understand it.'

So I went to see the agent and said, 'Look, I have got to come out.'

It took three years, as it does – I was in it for two years and then it took three years to get out, so I was exposed for five years – and I got out a few months before the whatsit hit the fan. That was her instinct. It was not an understanding of financial markets, it was just, 'You are committing money and you do not know what the risk is. That doesn't seem like a good idea to me.' And she was absolutely right.

Until recently I was chairman of 'Business in the Community', and had been for about five years. I have been very visible doing things in the work/life balance area at Reed, the Pru and now at Sainsbury's. I was involved for three and a half years with the government's New Deal, and that is very much about getting people who have children back to work. I am on Peter Ellwood's group for the DfEE on family work/life balance – I am one of the founder members of that group. Sainsbury's has historically done lots of good work in this field over the years. When I was a non-executive director on the board at Boots for eight years I chaired their corporate social responsibilities committee. Women return-ing to work, and part-time working and job-sharing were key issues and I helped push them quite hard. Boots developed some very good schemes. So I think people are aware I believe these areas to be important.

For relaxation I love going to the opera and ballet, and I am on the board of the Royal Opera House to fund-raise for them, so that ties in. I enjoy friends. We still have a lot of friends we have had for a long time. I enjoy spending time with the family. I enjoy sailing and now I have a bigger boat that has got a satellite phone on it I can always be reached if there is a real problem. That allows me to relax, curiously!

There is another aspect of work/life balance that is coming to the fore, which is not about children. It is about older parents, or relatives who are in some way disabled. It is only just beginning to dawn on us – as more and more of us are affected by the experi-ence – that with people living longer and with advances in medicine, with people recovering from illnesses and taking a long time to go through old age, that the strain on any family member coping with all that is immense. If you couple that with the demographic changes of more dispersed families, more single households, and more women at work, you get a combination of things that unexpectedly puts a lot of pressure on people at work. The time when you decide to have children is usually planned or discussed. The time at which an elderly relative suddenly fails or falls ill is unpredictable, and therefore much more difficult to manage. This is hitting people in their fifties and sixties, even people in their late forties, with parents in their seventies, or eighties and nineties. One of my female colleagues had a terrible time last year with a dying father, and now has a mother who has been very ill. If you are a two-career family, with four parents alive, things can be extremely difficult.

When I go to church it helps me relax and reflect on things. But I find the same effect from going to opera or ballet or going sailing. I am a communicant member of the Church of England but not terribly active. On the occasions when I go, I do get some comfort. But because there are other things that give equal relief, churchgoing does not drive me as hard as it drives some other people.

Something that is more important to me – it sounds corny and old-fashioned – is that I believe in putting something back into society, and that is one of the reasons I did 'Business in the Community', and why I do some of the other things I do. I try to tailor them to be things that I enjoy doing, admittedly, but nobody much enjoys fund-raising and I did five years' fund-raising for the NSPCC. The group I led raised the money for the new NSPCC training centre. It was a new building, and it was going to make a big difference. It gave me enormous satisfaction. I was using my business skills and contacts for a purpose other than business. That gave me great pleasure. **"**

## Keeping Your Balance

- Discuss career changes with your partner. Your career changes change their lives too. And they will bring an independent, often far-sighted, perspective to the matter.
- Tell your partner about all serious financial commitments which may involve them. Take their advice seriously. If you do not finally follow it, explain why not. Both partners have an interest in all family money.
- Get involved with charities and organisations that allow you to put something back into society. At first sight this will take up more of your time and take you away from your family more than ever. But it will help you achieve a healthy mental balance – and your partner may well get involved as well before long.

# Chapter 10

## LORD HOLLICK

Clive Hollick is chief executive of United Business Media, having previously been a director and chief executive of several of its broadcasting and publishing subsidiaries. He is chairman of the South Bank Centre, a director of TRW and of Diageo, and has been a director of Hambros Bank, Logica and British Aerospace. He founded and is a trustee of the Institute for Public Policy Research, was a member of the Commission on Public Policy and British Business and is a director of Britain in Europe. He has been a special advisor to the President of the Board of Trade and to the Secretary of State for Trade and Industry, and an advisor to successive leaders of the Labour Party.

Clive Hollick was born in 1945, educated at Taunton School and Nottingham University, and is married with three daughters.

**"M**anaging the balance between work and personal life is an issue that needs to be tackled like any other issue in your business life. It is not an issue where you can make mistakes and then brush them aside. First of all you need to understand the time demands of your job. 'How much time is it going to take?', 'What are the travel requirements?' and 'What are the evening requirements?' Then you must match that against the demands of your family life and against your leisure time. You need to approach it in a methodical way. I must confess that it is something I did not pay particular attention to for quite a long time. Fortunately Sue, my wife, identified it as an important personal and family issue and from that point onwards – which was shortly after we got married and had children – I sought to tackle it as one would tackle any other problem: analyse it, evaluate the issues and then develop ways of balancing the competing demands for your time and energy.

I give full credit to Sue because she really laid down some important ground rules when we started to have our family. One was that the weekend was sacrosanct. She had a full-time job, as I did, and unless we took the clear decision to carve out the weekend for family time, it would be frittered away, and it would disappear. That was a defining decision. It occurred not because my instincts were to tackle it that way, but because Sue said, 'If you don't do this, our family life will be squeezed to the margins of our lives and that will be to the detriment of our children and also ourselves.'

Ever since getting married we have had a house in the New Forest where we go every weekend. We travel down on Friday afternoons and we come back on a Sunday evening, or sometimes on Mondays – so we are all together for the weekend. Because we are in a different place and enjoy a different lifestyle in the New

Forest, weekends provide the opportunity for family pursuits, relaxation and renewal. I do take business papers to the farm and I do make some phone calls. But if I settle in front of the computer or get stuck on the phone, then eyebrows and voices will be raised.

Your partner sees the impact on your life of the stress of working, and of the sheer number of hours that you put in, far more clearly than you do. You are swept along by it. You are excited by it. Many of us have the great good fortune to have jobs that we are passionate about and become very engaged in. And because we do, we suspend the normal checks and balances; you are really enjoying your work, you really want to go for it, and you are building something and travelling and doing deals and coming up with exciting new ideas· and working with a great team of people. It is very heady and you are totally absorbed. That is a great privilege, but the price you pay is that it can push the rest of your life right to the margin. Your partner sees that more clearly and certainly earlier than you do. Your partner will say, 'Well, I acknowledge you get a tremendous amount of pleasure and enjoyment out of that and, yes, it also brings home the bacon. So I will support you and I will acknowledge that we pay a price as a family for that – but so far and no further.' That has been the very important role Sue has played.

I discuss some of the bigger business issues with Sue. I do not discuss the day-to-day issues. When I arrive home neither Sue nor our daughters necessarily want to hear the ins and outs of my business life. But if there is a particularly important issue or development, then it is of interest to all of them. I am careful not to impose my passion for work on Sue, or on my daughters. There are other things at the top of the family agenda. Business issues can be incredibly boring to listen to – people drivel on about what they have done during the day – so you need to have a sense of proportion about it and not burden your family with business minutiae.

Every weekday I leave home just after seven and I arrive at the office by about twenty to eight, and I work until around six-thirty, sometimes earlier, sometimes later. On a Friday I try to get away earlier and catch the five o'clock train. In the week I would have evening functions to go to, and I try to go to the House of Lords – so I tend to have fairly busy evenings. As chair of London Arts, Sue has many evening events, and I accompany her one or two evenings a week. We always try and go to the cinema together on a Monday, and we go to the theatre or the opera regularly. We have one or two cultural evenings together every week and a business and a social dinner. That is Monday through Thursday, and Friday we are in the country.

Unexpected events do interrupt the schedule. But there are certain events in the calendar particularly for one's children, ranging from the school play to going through their performance with their teachers, sports days and helping with academic projects which are scheduled in the calendar – and they are sacrosanct. I believe that I would score well on attendance on such occasions. When we lived in the United States and I had just been appointed to the board of the National Bus Company I had to attend my first board meeting. As a result I missed a party that we were hosting at our house in the USA. Sue was upset about that, and I felt really bad about it. From that point onwards I resolved that nothing would take precedence over such family and social occasions. I suspect everybody has had similar experiences – where you have done something and thought 'Oh my God, I wish I hadn't done that!'

On holidays I occasionally have had to spend time on the telephone but fortunately I have always worked with great people who can handle things in my absence. I keep in touch on the telephone and on my PC with e-mails. But I have never had to fly home from holiday.

When I started in the City back in 1968 I was not as diligent as I should have been. I had been working at Hambros Bank for some months before I discovered that I was supposed to work on a Saturday. So I was getting the life balance about right, but not the work balance! At that time there was a culture of 'You have got to be in the office. You have got to put in so many hours.' The presumption was that if you were not there and visible you were shirking. I can remember stories from those days about people who had a spare jacket to put on the back of their chair so it looked as though they had just gone down to the loo, when they were probably off for a very long lunch. Since then I have been fortunate. I am somebody who likes to work hard, and I have the energy to do so, but I am also by inclination somebody who likes to take time off and do other things. I am very conscious that if you get overburdened by your work you become stressed. Your enjoyment level diminishes and you become less effective. So I have been fortunate in working for chairmen and colleagues who also have the 'work hard, play hard' approach.

When I got into investment banking, I learned it was about getting the deal done, getting the new issue done, getting the fund-raising done, working all the hours and then having a damn good holiday, and that is how I look at things. People have got a job to do, they should work hard to do it, but if there is nothing to do then take time off. The culture of our organisation at United, like the culture of many companies, has changed quite markedly

over the last decade to one where we insist that people take their
full leave entitlement and do not regularly work late. I often have
conversations with colleagues when I say, 'You know, you should
take some time off.' I see it as part of my job – and certainly our
head of Human Resources makes it very clear that we insist on
achieving a good balance between work and home life. We are not
going to get the best out of our executives and professionals if we
do not take steps to help them get the balances right in their lives.
We have a vested interest in helping them balance their lives. We
now actively manage the issue of work/life balance throughout the
company.

There is always the anxiety that if you confide to one of your
colleagues, particularly to your superior, about a domestic problem, or a personal problem, it is somehow going to count against
you. We have taken the view at United that we need to provide a
safe haven where people can discuss these things. If they do not
want to discuss them with their direct superior, there are HR
professionals they can discuss such issues with. For a number of
years we have used mentoring schemes to help people, not only
to get new skills, but to address some of these personal issues.
They can do so on a confidential basis, and if the issue needs to
be discussed more widely then, with their agreement, it can be.
Maybe it is because so much of our business is in the United
States, where people are prepared to tell you quite openly how
they think and what they feel, that we are making steady progress
towards a culture where colleagues can talk one to the other about
their problems, and things are far more open. Everyone knows
there are problems which often are kept quiet. But a problem
shared can be a problem solved, and we all have an interest in
helping people to get through their problems. There is nothing

worse than being completely unsighted about somebody's problems and pushing them hard. We still have a long way to go but we are getting better. We have introduced a whole raft of measures from mentoring and training through to encouraging people to work from home for part of the week, to take sabbaticals, and encouraging parental leave, and flexible working. Our people know all of these options are available. And because of that people now feel they can talk about problems and say, 'I do need to take time off.' This morning somebody said to me 'Look, I am going to be late for that strategy meeting. I've got to take my son to school.' That is fine. That is not a problem. Ten years ago he might not have felt confident enough to say that.

Our colleagues in the United States have 'personal' days. You can take 'personals' and you do not have to say why; you just get up in the morning and say, 'I don't want to go into work today.' And OK, if there is nothing critical happening on that day you take a 'personal'. I think that is a smart way of legitimising the fact that some days you just do not feel like going to work, or something has cropped up in your private life and you want to deal with it without lengthy explanations.

For any company these policies are enlightened self-interest. We work in the media industry where people have strong views and express them strongly; they are creative and professional and demand to be treated as individuals. But people should be treated the same way regardless of the type of business they work in. You have to create an atmosphere where people feel comfortable. We have been through a period of tremendous change and challenge over the last couple of years and people have had to work extraordinarily hard for very long hours. They have been rewarded for it, but we have also encouraged them to take extended breaks.

That means that when you ask them to really step up to the plate again and give it 110%, they are more comfortable about doing so, because they know that they are going to be treated fairly when it comes to taking time off. To attract and retain top talent at all levels in the organisation, it is vital to help people manage the work/life balance and to deal with stress.

In business you come up against a lot of really crucial and tough decisions, and some of them are very difficult to make. By their nature they are complex and there are usually strong arguments on each side. I have found that if you work through them – not only by reading the documents but by talking to people, seeking advice: I really do like to get lots of input into these difficult decisions – and if you take your time over making the decision, then the level of stress can be reduced. That is not to say it is easy, but you follow this process and it helps you to get through without getting unduly stressed. You can get very stressed when there is a high level of uncertainty, or you are unsighted and you simply do not understand the situation sufficiently well and it spins out of control. Every chief executive and every person in a senior management position is by their very nature interested in the question, 'What can I control?' It is the things you cannot control that can be stressful. As you get more experienced you come to terms with what you cannot control.

My first chairman said to me, 'The biggest risk you can run in your business life is not taking risks. I do not mind if you fail on some decisions because if you are not failing, then you are not even trying.' That is a difficult lesson to drum into people. People are very defensive. If you take the decision in the light of all the evidence and you have gone through the proper processes – OK, you are going to get decisions wrong, but you are going, hopefully, to get a lot more of them right. But you have to learn to cope with inevitable failures, inevitable setbacks, when things go wrong and you feel a failure. No business career, no organisation, can be a linear road to success. You must come to terms with those setbacks and be able to put them into context and learn from them.

There have been a number of occasions when I faced a particularly difficult business decision. Some I shared with Sue and other friends, and others I gritted my teeth and went through alone. Today – as opposed to 20 years ago – I am far more comfortable about sharing them and talking to people about them, rather than bottling them up. I recall vividly setting up the Institute for Public Policy Research in 1986. I wanted to raise enough money to ensure it had at least a three-year life, but when we launched it I had a real concern that the money I had raised – we are talking a quarter of a million pounds – was not certain for the three years or more that I wanted it to be. The night before the launch of the thinktank I could not sleep, worried because we were saying that we had the money, whereas I had not yet raised it all. Not everything was buttoned down. It was to be such a public launch, and it was a particular passion of mine, which I had been nurturing for several years. I was really stressed. Experience has now taught me that if you set something up and get it running, and you get the initial funding in place, if it is successful it will take off and you do not need to worry about years three, four and five. But I was so concerned about it that I thought, 'Oh my God, this is going to be a major embarrassment if we do not get money in year three!' I did not share that fear with anybody.

Normally I sleep extremely well so I can remember the four or five occasions in my life – and the launch of the IPPR was one of them – when I was so stressed by a particular issue that was troubling me that it kept me wide awake. Sleep is a good indicator. I notice with some of my colleagues and friends that those who are blessed with the ability to sleep, and sleep deeply and regularly, have a real advantage. I have friends who just do not sleep very well and I think that puts additional stress on them during the working day.

I have mentioned the role Sue played in helping and encouraging me to strike the right balance between workload and the family. My past chairmen and colleagues have also played important roles. One of the things you learn working in investment banking is to operate in a very close team. While there is an element of competition, it is vital that you work together. You talk to each other about everything. One colleague who I worked with at that time had a far more relaxed attitude to life than I did, but he did not work any less hard. I watched him and thought, 'That is pretty cool. I'll try and be a bit more laid back, like him.' I am not sure if I succeeded. But you learn from others and, if you build close working relationships, people give you advice, and it comes back to the point that others see you much more clearly than you do yourself. One or two of my colleagues who have become good friends will say to me, 'Oh, you look a bit stressed. Are you worried?' Or 'You're not looking so well.' They spot it immediately. Whereas you looked in the mirror in the morning and thought, 'I look raring to go!'

I do a lot of business travelling. More than half our business is now in the United States so I spend a good chunk of my time over there. If I am going on a long trip I try to take a weekend out when I get there, maybe to go and see some friends, go scuba diving, play golf and go out in the evening to the theatre or the opera, so that it is not just all work. It can get very debilitating if you are going into meetings morning, noon and night. You go to some wonderful places. So you want to take some time out in the evenings and over the weekends.

The telephone bills when I am away are a testimony to the fact that I feel an element of guilt about being away. Sue has limited enthusiasm for accompanying me on business trips. She makes the point that she can stay at home and see me in the evening, which is what tends to happen on business trips. But she does often come to the States with me now, because one of our daughters lives there, and that brings an air of normality to evenings and weekends.

The curse of mobile phones and e-mails is that people know they can get hold of you at any time. When I think about the influence of e-mails, PCs and so on, on our personal lives, I remember my grandmother – I think it was in 1953 – buying a television set. She was concerned that it was going to disrupt and dominate all our lives so she insisted that it was only going to be watched on specific occasions, which she would stipulate. Any new technology that becomes an essential part of your life has the capability to become all-enveloping. But you then learn how to use it, and learn how to get the best out of it. For some people there is no moment of their life when they are not looking at their PC – well, that is a choice I would not make. Similarly, when you have got over the novelty factor, it is very easy to turn off the mobile phone and pick up the messages later.

One of the things I try to remember to say – when I do phone colleagues over the weekend, or in the evening – is 'Is it convenient?' because the telephone is a remarkably intrusive instrument. You think 'Oh, I'll just phone so-and-so.' You must respect their privacy. You do not phone people before nine o'clock in the morning at the weekend. You do not phone them in the evenings at the weekend, unless it is an emergency, and you give them the option of saying, 'Can I call you back. It's not convenient right now.' Mobiles are damn useful, but sometimes I see people using them on trains and think it has become an extension of their body and their being. I would rather read a book!

Since the early 1980s I have been involved in politics. I don't spend as much time as I would like on political matters because I have a demanding full-time job. In those areas where I have expertise I try to make a contribution. On issues of business policy, or an election campaign, I will commit a lot of my time and energy. I am not as diligent an attender in the House of Lords as I would like to be, but I have to manage my time and consider, 'How can I best make my contribution?' For the first year of the 1997 Labour government I was a special advisor in the Department of Trade and Industry. I agreed to take on the role on the basis of two hours a day. Two hours a day turned out to be an impossibility. The sheer volume of work was so great I had to give it up after about 15 months. I am also involved in charitable work and supporting various art organisations.

When you have a young family you do things you can share. When they are at home we ride in the New Forest, we play tennis, we walk, we all go skiing together, we go on safari, we go on cultural holidays. In London we go to the theatre, movies and gigs. Now our children have grown up, Sue and I have become enthusiastic golfers, a sport that is difficult to combine with a young family because it takes such a great chunk out of the day. From a business point of view, it is an opportunity to meet business colleagues and make new friends in a relaxed environment. It combines three things I like – it combines a pleasant social event, a walk in some of the most beautiful countryside, and the challenge of hitting a pesky little ball in the right direction.

One of the penalties we pay for being in the country at weekends is that our social life in London becomes a little truncated. We have a very close-knit group of friends we have stayed close to and – maybe it is just a function of age – we now meet old friends and acquaintances more than we used to. My circle of friends is a very important part of my life. They are people who work in a variety of quite different areas, not necessarily business. In fact only a few of my friends are in my business. I have a lot of political friends. And I have made some very good friends through working in television and the media. They are friends rather than business acquaintances. You want friends who have different views of the world and different perspectives, and Sue and I now have many friends in the States, and in other countries. I believe that having a mix of friends from different backgrounds who do different things and who have different areas of expertise, and who often come from different countries, enriches your enjoyment of life. It puts your own issues – coming back to the topic of work/life balance – into perspective. I would find it difficult if my social life simply mirrored my business life, discussing all the same issues, talking to all the same people.

Business is very stimulating but there are a lot of other things in my life that are equally stimulating. Energy is a finite resource, so you really have to think carefully because there are so many interesting and important things to do. The opportunity to make a contribution, to make a difference, is enormously satisfying and challenging. I often ask myself, 'How can I solve that?' 'How can I improve this?' I certainly push myself. If there is a challenge out there I am up for it. Whatever I do, whether it is in business or politics or working in the public sector or in a charity, I am always asking, 'How do we move this forward? What is the right policy? Can we be more creative? How do we attract the best people? How do we take advantage of this opportunity?' I really enjoy working with a team of people to achieve a common goal and getting to know each of them and trying to create the right environment for each of them to play their full part.

I am not a religious person. I see organised religion all too often being divisive and leading to grief and suffering in the name of one body claiming a superior set of values. I do feel that there is an important set of core human beliefs and ethical values, many of them religious in origin. There is an important spiritual element to life but it is personal, to be shared with family and friends and not dictated by organised religion. I enjoy reading about ideas, discussing ideas and being intellectually curious. The arts and the creative world play an important role in my life.

Successful businesses are important to society. They provide jobs, they provide the economic wherewithal, they provide emotional and creative sustenance and they provide the services and goods that people want and need. That is all for the greater good. One of the political battles in which I have played a part is helping to shift Labour and the left from the view that business was bad, business was exploitative, to the view that business is a vital part of a successful society. Of course, you have got to curb excess and exploitation – but enterprise is a good thing.

Looking at myself I see two conflicting and contradictory elements. One is that I feel I am inherently a rather lazy person. This may sound odd, but I believe it. It probably comes from somewhere deep in my childhood. I often feel I should be doing more. I am constantly ambitious to learn more. And there is a lot more I can do that involves working with people and organisations. I also believe private time is important. Time by yourself to think, to reflect, to read. Work and evening events sadly reduce the amount of time devoted to reading. I read about a chief executive who reads two novels a week and who reads for an hour before he goes to sleep each night, and I thought, 'My God, that's impressive.'

Above all I want to emphasise the need for a systematic and thoughtful approach to the complex issues of balancing work with your home and social life. It is a question of turning good intentions into a programme that can be made to work. For many of us there are many good intentions and a lot of talk but not enough action. This issue is now firmly on the individual and corporate agenda. Companies and organisations need to find a way of dealing with it, and the trade unions have an important role to play too. Politicians provide the worst kind of example. I know very few politicians who are able to balance their work and home lives effectively – they are trapped by their jobs, they are prisoners of their jobs. As a result they are less effective than they could otherwise be. Leadership is required in this area. It is important that we move from words to actions and all organisations and individuals give a high priority to getting the balance right. **"**

## Keeping Your Balance

- Create your own 'personal' days by holding back a week or two of your holiday entitlement and taking it a day or two at a time. It may not be possible, as in America, to take days off on the spur of the moment, but it can always be done with a little advance notice.

- Make friends with people from many walks of life, outside your own industry. This will enhance your work/life balance by providing you with broader, stimulating perspectives.
- Go out with your partner at least one evening every week.
- Do as you would be done by: do not telephone business colleagues at truly unreasonable times – such as very early or late at weekends – and always ask whether it is convenient, or whether they would prefer to call you back later.
- Others can often see our problems more clearly than we can ourselves. Ask close friends how they think you are handling your work/life balance: do they think you could be handling things better?

# Chapter 11

---

# HELEN ALEXANDER

Helen Alexander is chief executive of the Economist Group, which she joined in 1985. She is a non-executive director of Northern Foods and is a trustee of the Tate Foundation. She is a former director of BT plc. Previously she worked with Duckworth and Co. and with Faber and Faber.

Helen Alexander was born in 1957 and educated at St Paul's Girls' School, Hertford College, Oxford, and INSEAD (MBA). She is married and has one daughter and two sons.

**"I**t is always tough, however much you plan. You cannot plan your work/life balance for five years ahead. You can plan the general circumstances, to make sure they are right. After that, it is short-term planning, reacting to things as they happen; sometimes one puts the family first, sometimes the job: it depends on the circumstance completely. That is true both for me and for my husband. We are a partnership.

Let me give an example. Last summer the Economist Group was involved in a major, very important deal. I went to New York for two weeks and we were due to close the paperwork by the end of the first week – the middle of the first week, actually. We did not close for the next ten days, and by then I was due to go away with the family. As we were very near to closing, but there was detailed work still to be done, the finance director flew out and carried the baton on for me, while I went off on holiday with the family. We went to a remote part of America where they could not phone me because there were no proper connections. So I telephoned them. I phoned in twice a day, to keep in touch and see what was going on. The following week I flew from holidaying back to the East Coast for one day, and then went back to join the family on the West Coast again after the meeting. So that was business encroachment into my family life – but I kept it to the minimum, definitely the minimum.

There are other occasions when I have come back to meetings and presentations and I am not sure with hindsight that it was worth it. One of our clients asked for me to be at a lunch, so I came back from a skiing holiday and afterwards thought that the lunch was fine, but I am not sure one more person's presence at a big lunch is ever all that critical. My husband and I work very, very hard to make sure that both of us never have to be called back simultaneously, and fortunately it does not happen that much, if at all. Sometimes I avoid coming back, by staying behind and joining the family later. Both my husband and I work hard. If I have to work he can handle everything. The reciprocal is also true. If he has to work, then I do the same. We take responsibility for the household supplies and cooking equally; one week I am in charge of all that, the next week he is. We have done it like that for 17 years. We split the school runs between us, too.

By half-past eight I am in the car working and I am physically in the office at nine, but that first half-hour is concentrated work. About half the days of the week I leave work at six o'clock to be home by six-thirty, and the other days my husband is the one that has to be home by six-thirty. We divide that pretty rigidly 50/50, and our assistants plan whose 'late evening' it is going to be. If I have a late meeting then he gets home early and vice versa, and over time it works out evens. If I am travelling he may have to do five evenings on the trot and then when I get back I might do five: it equalises itself out over a few months. That is all part of our 'family system'. The system is that one of us should always, always be at home, or wherever, with the children. We have three children, so we have to organise five people's lives. We all need organising, all need emotional support, all need practical support, the children need driving around, they need things done for them. That is all part of having a 'family system'. And so is having excellent support – notably our excellent nanny. We three adults regard ourselves as a triangle, each axis of which is important.

Even when I am home by six-thirty that is not the end of the working day. Typically, if we are at home, I start work again at about ten. Three or four nights a week – probably four – I do ten until midnight, either talking to America or working on the computer at home where I have a link into the office. I work Friday nights and Sunday nights, but have a complete break between for the weekend. I almost never have to do weekend meetings. And I do not live with my laptop permanently switched on, as some people do. At a parents' meeting at our daughter's school there was a guy wandering round with his laptop on. It was a tragic sight. I do not know what he was doing. But that I would not do.

When either my husband or I have a big issue, a long-term issue, to deal with then we talk to each other about it, but each of us has our own life and running two is more difficult than running one, so we do not have time to discuss the small stuff. On the whole his business life and entertainment are his, and mine are mine. But we certainly share everything important.

I do not know whether the constant pressure makes me stressed. Stress is a funny word. I feel very able to switch off. But when there are big things going on they sit there, in the back of the mind. I get out of London every weekend, and that helps a lot. But I do not have much time for leisure activities. I go to the gym, I run – but none of that takes very long. Watching our children play sports or listening to them in a concert is a pleasure. The idea that we might, for example, send our children off to summer camp seems bizarre to us both, frankly.

There are occasional exceptions, but most of my travelling is done in the middle of the week and that is quite deliberate. I was listening to the radio yesterday and a pop star was talking about how she had a young child and how much she had to travel, and she said, 'I try not to be away very much. I try never to be away for more than six weeks at a time.' I thought, 'Blimey!' Normally the worst that happens for me is that I get back at dawn on Saturday morning after a week away. And I have never flown home for a children's event and then gone back again, although I could imagine doing so. Instead I have geared my departure and return times around the children's events to make sure they fit in with my husband's and my family system, and he does the same.

When I am travelling I try to pack in an enormous amount. One of John Harvey Jones' books said that if you are abroad and the company is paying for you to stay at an expensive hotel, and have an expensive flight, and to be away from your desk, then you absolutely owe it to the company to pack your day morning, noon and night with work. That is how I run my time abroad.

Coping with all these issues is a fact of life. The Economist Group is a good place in that sense. My predecessor David Gordon was very conscious of such issues – he hired women including senior women quite deliberately, and made things possible for them. The Economist Group understands, and says flexibility is important and it is one of the things we can offer. Not being a huge operation helps because you can adapt to individuals a bit more. It is absolutely known that I think senior people ought to make it possible for their staff to achieve a proper work/life balance. It is impossible to say to them, 'You have to let people have time off', because sometimes the team around the person cannot then cope. But the senior people must be able to show that they have tried. It is not one rule for me, or for senior people, and a different rule for everybody else. I absolutely do not expect people to be available at all hours of the day and night.

On the other hand it is important for people to know that they can reach me at any time, and then to use that knowledge responsibly. It would be irresponsible in my view for me to say, 'I am uncontactable. You can't find me.' So that is never the case. When I go out for a meeting my diary shows where I am and what the phone number is there. That would be true 365 days a year if necessary. It is partly an emergency procedure system. If I am travelling, my husband has my full itinerary. That is the system for both of us. It is always possible for us to make contact, so we do so responsibly.

There have been occasions when I have had to drop work and deal with a family issue, but that is the sort of thing I tend to get on with and then dismiss. You just weigh up the balance of importance at the time. We were in an audit committee meeting – audit committees are reasonably formal twice-a-year occasions – and I got called out and told my son had broken his arm. My reaction was to phone my husband and go back to the audit committee. My reaction to shock is usually denial. Life must go on as normal unless it is so awful that it just can't. My husband is completely different. He will say, 'I'll be right there. Don't worry.' I wish I was more like him in that way, because it is good. It does not make me feel constantly guilty, but there are instances where I think, 'Oh damn, I wish I had done that.' But it is not underlying, permanent guilt. I was having an important business telephone conversation with somebody the other day and he said, 'I am sorry, I've got to go. The hearse for my mother's funeral has just arrived!' We all just have to cope with situations like that.

There is no question that the issues of work/life balance, though not at the top, are now rising high on the agenda. They are mainly being brought on by younger people – that is by people under 50, as opposed to over 50. It is clearly something younger people take into account when they are changing jobs, and they raise it when they are being interviewed. So it is important to them. And that is a good thing. It is not really a gender thing, not a male/female issue; it is not just an issue for women. It is an issue for both. That is really important. I am thinking for example of paternity leave. We had a finance controller who we actually had to send home after his first child was born. He was not in a state to be here! It was not to do with exhaustion; it was his mental and emotional state, and you could see it. I am one of the few people here who often turns up for work at half-term! Men and women here take time off at half-term almost equally.

I learned a lot on a course I took when I was doing an MBA at INSEAD. It was called 'Women in Management' and it got me to read a body of writing on women in organisations, with real case studies. And since then I have continued to be interested in stuff that the Industrial Society has done, for example. It does not provide rules, but it does provide guidelines. There is potentially a regulatory context here too, and being aware of the issues is part of my job.

If you are in a position at the top of a company, you must have been ambitious to get there. But I do not think of myself as particularly ambitious, not compared with the people I meet now. My mother asks me why I keep driving myself. I do not know the answer. It is partly because I am quick with basic stuff. We recently did assessments and one of the pieces of feedback was, 'You are very quick with handling stuff' – that is good – but 'You expect others to be just as quick' – that is bad. Give them a break, was the message; lighten up because you are too demanding, and in most cases that is not fair and not fruitful. There is some truth in the generalisation that women work harder because their education says, 'Be master of the detail and get it all done.' So you make sure you have your homework done, and it is unthinkable to be skimming board papers as you go into the board meeting. Women's education has a lot to answer for.

While people are now starting to focus on the problems of caring for children, they are not yet thinking about the problems of caring for elderly family. One of my colleagues is driven by the problem of having elderly parents, and needing time off for them, needing to be able to create the support systems that allow him simultaneously to be able to work properly and look after them. This is increasingly important. It is a result of a demographic shift, I guess. There are a whole set of issues that people just do not talk about much at work and some of them need to be allowed to come out into the open. Over ten years ago – a long time ago, I know – my father died and I rang in and told my secretary, and she kept it a secret, much to my dismay. Today I find that odd – but how *do* you treat people who have recently been bereaved? How do you treat people who have recently had miscarriages? How do you treat people who are undergoing fertility treatment? There is piles of stuff that does not get talked about at work. Maybe that is not exactly a work/life balance issue but it is certainly about the relationship between personal and business life.

At the Economist Group we do not have an advice line or whatever, although there has been a lobby here saying that it would be a good idea. The tougher cultural point is: ought people to be grown up and deal with all this themselves, without us nannying them, or should we provide counselling and things like that? It is hard to know how much to get involved, but if you do not care at all you lose good people. We could lose a lot of people if we did not behave properly. Nowadays, when people are making a choice about whether or not to come to work here, they often ask pertinent questions, which touch on work/life balance. If you did not have some answers you would look a real dummy. And you would lose the people, the good people.

When I was younger I used to quite deliberately organise calls with the USA in the ten o'clock to midnight period. I have stopped doing that because it is much more intrusive at home than doing other kinds of work. I do not mind being rung up myself at night, but on the whole I now try to avoid calling others at night. There is no question everybody works very hard at the Economist Group – from breakfast meetings onwards – but you must make sure people have time to think. That is increasingly on my agenda because it is something I myself do not find comes naturally. Creating time to think has to be planned, too.

Of course I enjoy it all, though I am not sure I would classify it as fun. I do think about work a lot. I have one colleague who, if you said, 'Are you enjoying yourself? Are you enjoying your job at the moment?' simply would not get it. He would not understand what the question was about. He would say he finds work interesting and stimulating and remunerative and all sorts of things, but not enjoyable.

Do I want to change my life? If I did, then I would – and I am not doing so right now. **99**

## Keeping Your Balance

- Create a 'family system'. If your partner is at work too, correlate your diaries at the start of each week to ensure one of you is always available for the children. (This is doubly easy if your diaries are computerised.)
- Let your partner, as well as your PA, know how you can be contacted in an emergency.
- Share organisational necessities – school runs and the like – equally with your partner. If one of you gets behind with the balance as a result of travelling, or special work pressure, make up the shortfall later. Above all, always make sure both of you think the share is fair.

# Chapter 12

## JOHN CLARE

John Clare is group chief executive of the Dixons Group, which he joined as marketing director in 1985. Formerly he was marketing and business development director of the Ladbroke Group, which he joined after having started at Mars as a trainee.

John Clare was born in 1950, and educated at Great Yarmouth Grammar School and Edinburgh University. He is married with two sons.

66 The marketplace and business life are more and more competitive, more and more challenging, moving faster and faster. That creates many demands on your time, and it has got worse over the years. Just as importantly it creates many more demands on your mental space, and that too has got worse over the years. Things that contribute to all this include the introduction of

computers, the relaxation of competition rules, the greater open-
ness of business. It is a much more dynamic, challenging environment than 20 years ago, and it is still noticeably changing year by
year. This sets challenging questions for individuals, when they
come to manage their time and their mental space, and want to
bring up kids and do lots of other things as well.

If you are going to get the balances right there has to be an
element of planning, but it is not detailed planning in a business-
type planning sense. There are no spreadsheets, no allocations of
time, no managing a diary through a personal life as well as a
business life. But in my mind there have always been rules and
guidelines to which I have tried to work. Sometimes that has been
possible and sometimes it has not. I have tried to keep work away
from weekends – by work I mean office work and meetings, that
sort of work. Being in a retail business you spend a lot of weekends in stores and I have brought my kids up dragging them
around stores and shops on a Saturday morning. But that involved
the family so it was also family time. I try to keep overnights away
down to two a week. Two or three times a year I have to do the
States and Japan, but in a normal week I try to get home to sleep
three nights during the week. There is a structure that I am well
aware of and that I try to stick to. But it is a broad structure, not a
detailed plan.

I take my holidays and I demand everyone here takes their
holidays. For all senior management I insist they take at least one
holiday of two or three weeks in a year. It is checked off and I keep
an eye on it. If people are going to work hard when they are here
they should take their holidays. Having said that, when I am on
holiday – and I take one holiday of three weeks a year in the
summer – I am on the phone to the office every single day. Unless

something dramatic is happening it is a ten- or 15-minute conversation. I want to know the sales figures, and that there are no special problems. In my position I have to know what is happening in all our markets. I have to know what is happening with the share price. I have to know what is happening with sales, by product group at least. So there are some ticks needed, and if it is all ticks you can ring off quite quickly and relax until the next morning. It would not be possible in my position, nor for most people at the top of this organisation, to take a holiday and not stay in touch regularly. I do it every day but for others it would be every two or three days, at least.

Occasionally over the years, I have found myself taking a holiday when a deal was going on or when crucial things were happening. Since joining Dixons I have only twice come back from a holiday, and abandoned it in midstream. One was when we had a bid against us and another was when we were doing an acquisition.

It is difficult to say what hours I work, because it depends on what you mean by work. Work is a mental state as well as a physical state, and it involves offices and shops but it also involves dinners and relatively social occasions, which you are actually doing because you have to meet banks or suppliers and represent the company, or just network.

In the middle of the night at home, at about three or four in the morning, I get the sales figures for the previous day. I am asleep, but I get them sent wherever I am in the world, so if my secretary knows I am in the Far East or overnight in Finland the figures will arrive there in the middle of the night or the equivalent time. As the mainframe computer is churning through the numbers, it sends me a summary. When I wake up in the morning, as I am shaving and washing, I will know the sales figures line by line and will be starting to chew over what they mean, and what we should do as a result, or not do as a result. I will know what has happened within each of the retail chains. I will know what has happened within each of the key geographic regions, and I will know what has happened to the key products.

So by the time I get into the car at a quarter to seven I can start phoning people – I do not usually phone before seven. I ring around and talk to people about what all the figures imply, or indeed whatever else is happening. I am an hour's drive from the office at that time in the morning so I am physically in my office by about eight. The whole cycle starts an hour earlier on a Monday because Monday is the big day in retailing, for the previous week. Then I leave work by about six. I do not leave late, but it is seven o'clock or later before I get home. That is a 12-hour day, home to home. Two or three evenings a week I will be out until 11 or 12 o'clock.

I rarely work at papers when I am at home. But telephone calls can still be made and telephones still ring. I never ring anybody at home unless it is an emergency. I do not continue the workday once I have got out of the car at home, unless it is exceptional. I try very hard not to take work home so that when I do get in I am with the family and switched off as much as I can be. Yes, things happen from time to time and, yes, we have to do deals, and I have taken telephone calls in the middle of the night on occasion, but they are the exception rather than the rule.

I have always tried to attend things like school parent events, plays and sporting events – some of those are at the weekends anyway. Some I missed, but most I went to. You try to get to them when you can. If I missed one or two, I missed one or two, but not too many. The ones that you do have to miss, and it does happen – I do not know anybody who has been able to do every-thing they have wanted to – will cause a bit of a family crisis, and you have to accept it and get over it. I will look back and remem-ber all the times I was there, and my wife or the kids will look back and remember all the times I was not there, but that is the way of memories.

When you are younger, sometimes you can explain to your boss you need time off, sometimes you cannot. You take a judgment on that. If somebody now came to me and asked, by and large I would be considerate and understanding if it was important enough. But I do not think I have any senior managers who would come to me and ask for time off for a sports day on a Wednesday, or for an open evening if something important was happening in the business. If somebody came to me and said, 'The school has just been on the phone. My son is about to be expelled. It's a crisis. I have to get there', I would be sympathetic and let them go. Look-ing back, I cannot recall a time when I have myself asked for time off like that, other than for an illnesses or if something serious had happened. And I would not expect others to do it unless it was serious.

There was an occasion when I was working for Mars, where I worked for the first 12 years of my business life. The first time I was ever asked to personally present to Forrest Mars himself – he was in the UK, I had prepared the presentation, and was going to present to him for the first time in my life – that very day, just before my presentation, I heard my wife had miscarried. The mis-carriage had already happened, and I did the presentation, then got to the hospital as fast as I bloody well could and tried to balance the two crises. But as far as my wife was concerned I was about an hour late, and as far as the company was concerned I ducked out early. The things coincided and I had to make a tough call. What you do in circumstances like that depends on individuals rather than companies or policies.

My philosophy now is that if people are working very hard and are very committed, there are times when you have to give something back. That is a general philosophy that is easier to preach than to practise. On an issue-by-issue basis you will come across some people that try to take you for granted, and if they come with yet another request you will be more inclined to say, 'No, get lost.' They are people that you do not anyway regard as hard workers, and you probably ought to get them out of the business, so you have less sympathy for their requests. But the greater the demands the company puts on you when you are 100% at work, the more the company ought to be inclined to give you a bit of space if you need it.

These issues are more difficult for women, and we discuss them a lot here at Dixons with the women who are senior managers. If women want to have a family there is a break in their life you have to accommodate, and if they are in senior management the accommodation of that break is very difficult, whether it be for three months – in retail three months can be an eternity – or for a couple of years, which some of them would like. When the women come back, having young families, they have a maternal instinct, which is different from a paternal instinct. Much as we might try and legislate for them to overlap, or try and change habits so that they overlap, I do not think society is there yet. Some individuals are there. Some individual families might be there. But more often than not if the child at school has come down with German measles or broken a leg it is the mother who will be telephoned first. We have to accommodate that. The mother brings the children into the world and then brings them up in their early formative years with a closer relationship than the father, which makes it very difficult for women to be in senior management positions, particularly given the demands of a retail business, through those years of their lives. If they do not have children that is a different matter. Many women in senior management have chosen not to have children, but those who do have a difficult time.

I do not have personal experience of lots of industries, but I know retailing is hugely demanding in terms of time, particularly mental time, and Dixons' businesses are at the very, very fastest end of retailing. If you are not in touch here, in half an hour you can miss significant things happening. Most manufacturing businesses work in a different way. Most public service businesses are different. And indeed some retail businesses are different. Grocery is always thought to be a very fast-moving retail sector, but they plan three months ahead and they have promotions that last for a month. We change 200 prices a day, and if you are responsible for product categories where that has got to happen and you are out of touch, by the time you get round to it, it is too late.

Having said that, I do not regard a lot of what we do as hard work, certainly not physically hard relative to some businesses. It is mentally all-consuming. You absolutely have to be consumed by what goes on in the business. We look for people that first and foremost are very competitive, and second are prepared to get highly involved with the business at a high level of detail, at least in senior management positions. CEOs of other companies might stay well away from the detail of what is going on, and feel they are only responsible for strategy and acquisitions. In certain businesses that is highly relevant. In ours it is not. At the top of the organisation you have to have operational flare, and you have to be very competitive. Whether or not you call that hard work depends on where you are coming from.

It is stressful, but to do well here you have got to be the sort of person that does not worry. If you are a worrier you will not last ten minutes. From time to time we have recruited worriers and by lunchtime on the first day we will know we have made a mistake and they will know they have made a mistake. There are a vast number of decisions being taken all the time, and if you are the sort of person who wants to think about taking a decision, and then worry about it after you have taken it, you will be dead. You will get buried by the complexity. So senior managers here are not worriers, but stress can be caused by more than just worry. There are lots of variables involved. Stress can be caused by pressure of time and by all sorts of things. Stress happens at the top of any business and it happens at the top here, but we try as best we can to get people who are not going to cave in under the pressure.

When people start here I tell them, 'Never be frightened of taking a decision. Never be frightened of getting it wrong. If you are taking the number of decisions you need to take in this business you will get a third of them wrong – and that will be a bloody good track record. What is absolutely important is for you to know it was wrong before your boss finds out it was wrong, and by the time your boss finds out it was wrong you have corrected it. The first thing to do every morning is check the results of the decisions you took yesterday. In retail you usually know on a day-by-day basis. So check yesterday's decisions and change the ones that did not work. Then sort out what the opportunities are for today and create another load of decisions. By the time your boss has got round to your bit of the business you have moved on. I do not have any problem accepting that if somebody else is in a better position to take a decision than me, then let them take it. If I have to take the decision, I will take it. Retailing encourages decisiveness: take the decision and move on.'

So it is clear and obvious to employees from very early on what the environment is like, and people have to fit into it quickly. You cannot throw the environment at people slowly. You cannot build them up to it. They have to build up to it themselves. Again, when people come here I say, 'It will be six months before you know what is going on. It will take six months because your brain is going to move faster and faster, faster and faster. You will not be aware of it but until it is moving at the same speed as the business, you will not see things clearly. And then it will hit you. It hits you very suddenly. One day you will come in to work and things will be in focus and you will not quite know why, and then you are there.' For the first six months it can be very, very bewildering. But the business cannot accommodate people slowly. You get thrown in the deep end. We have had some fairly spectacular failures. I joined this business as marketing director because my predecessor had a nervous breakdown and disappeared, and he had only been in the business a few weeks. He just could not take it, so they went back to the market and started to recruit again. That was 17 years ago. We are getting much better at selection now, but still you have people who cannot cope. They throw up their hands in horror and say, 'This is not what I thought it was going to be like. I can't take this, thank you very much.'

But once this business gets into your bones and your blood you are there. Senior management here in the main are long-serving – up to 20 years and more. If you like it, you love it. There is nothing else quite as attractive, exhilarating and stimulating. And if you love it and you are confident and bright and competitive, you will do well. It is much more to do with your personality than with your educational background or your intellectual powers or any of those sorts of things.

If you are going to get to the top of the business it is going to demand time and mental energy, so there has to be a huge amount of understanding from your partner. If that is not there either the partnership collapses or the business life collapses, and there are plenty of examples of both. Your partner is critical. Your partner is involved. My wife has spent trips wandering around stores with the kids. Over the years we have pulled together team events here, and my wife has held social events and been involved with the partners of the senior managers. It is an active role, and if you do not get that support it can be a lot tougher.

At the top of Dixon's we have quite a strongly united team of about 20 people – I could take it another couple of layers down and say 100 people – where my wife would know their partners and she would know their family situations. A lot of that has resulted from social occasions she has been responsible for organising and helping to run. If everybody knows everybody else and they have socialised together, the benefits rub off for everybody. There is less abrasiveness. There is less friction. There will still be issues that need to be resolved and there will still be differences of opinion, but you find solutions more easily if people have more understanding of each other. The team at the top here has held together now for about a dozen years and my wife has played a big, big part in making all that happen. And though I do not discuss every detail of the business with her – that would be impossible – I do talk to her about strategic issues.

Retailing is a situation where mentally you do not ever switch off, and you live with that. You either enjoy it or it is a burden. If you enjoy it, it is not a burden, it does not matter. Do I enjoy hearing complaints from customers on social occasions? No, I don't enjoy hearing complaints but it goes with the territory. If I am sitting at a dinner this evening I will be worried about today's sales. And if I am grocery shopping at the weekend, I will be looking for ideas from the way other retailers are doing things. You never stop. Fortunately I do not feel a need to have time on my own. It does not matter to me. Every night when I am at home I walk the dog before going to bed, which gives me half an hour to calm down before sleep. I do not consciously say, 'I must have some time of my own to relax', but I suppose it is in a way relaxing. I know others who need a lot of solitary time, a lot more than I do.

This business is itself a complete and utter way of life. It absorbs you. Is it of benefit to society? Yes, it is of benefit to society but it is not a charity-type benefit. It is not a welfare-type benefit and I am certainly not running this business because I believe my role in life is to run a charity. If I did, there would be a whole lot of other things that would come much higher up the list than selling electrical goods. Nonetheless we are running a business that helps technology develop, that is important, and we are exposing customers to technology efficiently and productively, and at the right prices. Is that good rather than bad? The answer is 'Good'. What we do is honest, ethical and sensible, and over the years society benefits from having retailers like us around. And it is very important to me not to do anything that is harmful to society. It is also very important for this business not to do anything that is harmful to society. There are some quite significant issues here.

We import products from China and Taiwan and there are difficult issues concerning labour in those countries. It is very important to me to be ethical and conduct the business honestly and openly. But is it a prime motivator that I work for Dixons because it is benefiting society? No. What really motivates me is the competitive and fast-moving nature of retailing. Those are the bugs that get you.

We as a business, and we as a nation, cannot stay isolated in the world. Technology exists and people have to use it. The whole of the business machine worldwide today is moving faster and faster and sometimes you wonder whether the whole thing is going to implode. If it ever does, hopefully I will not be at the wheel by then! Meanwhile competitive industry becomes more and more intense. At the very top of business, life-cycles are probably going to become shorter. People will stay in jobs for a shorter length of time. You are seeing it now. Top business people become advisors or non-executive directors so they can use their experience without being in the front line any more. And when it comes to technology, you have to manage it and not let it manage you. Effectively and constructively used technology will help you manage the balance between your business and your private life.

I am ambitious, but wherever I have been in life my ambition has been to get the next job up. As soon as I have got into a job I have thought, 'How do I get the next one?' And for much of your life you do not have the ability to worry about jobs beyond that, because you do not actually know what they do, or know only vaguely. So I am ambitious in that sense. I have never been completely content with where I am. But I am not the sort of person who said, 'By the time I am 45 I have to be a director of a public company or else I have failed' – and you come across people like that. My advice to others is always limit your ambition. Limit your ambition to the next job because that is the one you will be able to do better than your boss, if you observe and manage the position carefully. And as soon as you can do it better than your boss, work at getting it. And the best way to get it is to get somebody underneath you who can do your job better than you. That has served me well, up to now.

Money has not been the driver, either. Having enough – whatever enough is, and enough becomes a slightly different figure over the years – to live comfortably, and to not have to worry about money is important. I spent the early years of my life worrying about money, as a lot of young marrieds do, and I am very glad to be out of that sort of worry. Money gives you a comfortable life and makes a lot of this worthwhile, but money is not a key motivator for me. I would not go and work for another company just because they offered me a fortune more than I get here. That has happened, frequently. I find it an interesting paradox, in a retail business that is all about how much you have in the till at the end of the day – but I distance that from what my own pay is at the end of the month.

I started at Mars and that was very fortunate. They were great trainers of people in the early 1970s – as far as I know they still are – so my first weeks in business were at a sales training school attending courses and learning how to sell. Mars were very good at sending you on management development courses and they had good internal training departments as well. There were also people who helped me get promotion. It was part of the way the business ran. The business was constantly expanding and growing and looking to pull people through, so the managers around you were trying to pull you through, by giving you whatever help you needed. But the further up you go, the more you are left to your own devices. By the time I got into Dixons I was already a marketing director so here I have been more on the dishing-out end than on the receiving end. We are doing a hell of a lot more today to help our young people than we did when I started. We now put people on development courses and have internal programmes of management development.

Most of them are technical courses, and in retailing 'technical' is not about products but is about selling skills, marketing skills, training skills, buying skills and negotiating skills. Then there are the management courses about how to be a better manager, where there is quite a lot of emphasis on lifestyles, and on business and personal life balances. They teach you how you can be a better manager of your people, and how you develop those skills – social skills in a management perspective – over time.

Looking back, I would not want to change anything of significance, to make any major shift in the balance between my personal and business lives, if I did it all over again. I am reasonably happy. **99**

## Keeping Your Balance

- Get your partner to help with the organisation of business social events, so they can get to know your colleagues (and their partners).
- In several types of business – especially retailing and some other service businesses – your partner and children can get involved with you at the weekend, visiting shops or competitors' operations. If so, try to make it fun.

- Some business sectors, and retailing is one of them, inevitably eat into your personal time more than others (even if you do not receive sales figures at three o'clock in the morning!). This is the way things are, and you cannot change them – but in every sector some organisations are more sensitive to work/life issues than others.

# Chapter 13

# SIR MICHAEL PERRY, GBE

Michael Perry is currently chairman of Centrica plc and a member of the Supervisory Board of Royal Ahold. He is President of the Marketing Council, chairman of the Shakespeare Globe Trust, chairman of the Oxford University Faculty Board for Management and vice-president of the Liverpool School of Tropical Medicine. He is also a trustee of Glyndebourne Arts Trust, the Leverhulme Trust and Dyson Perrins Museum Trust. He retired as chairman of Unilever plc in 1996 after 39 years of Unilever service.

Born in 1934, Michael Perry was educated at King William's College, Isle of Man, and St John's College, Oxford.

He is married with a son and two daughters.

**"T**here has been a considerable quickening of the pace of life in recent years – and probably throughout one's career as one gets more senior. The idea that as one gets older and more senior the opportunity to look down benignly on those beavering away below is a myth, which very soon gets dispelled by reality. As one gets more senior in a business inevitably there is more managing to do. But in my case there is a sort of built-in, almost physiological requirement to create space and create some sort of balance as compensation for periods of pressure. People have different ways of dealing with pressure. For me there is this need suddenly to distance myself, and I have done that by hurling myself into a whole series of things that were not business-related.

I developed rules in relation to the strict controls I put on the preservation of family life. The maintenance of a secure family base was an almost instinctive priority, and I always worked on the basis that my work was about providing for my family, and the family took priority over everything else. Had I been faced with a situation in which something had to give, in that set of priorities, I would always have sacrificed the business side in order to preserve the other, so there was no doubt what I was working for in my own mind – though it was never tested in that way.

I was very fortunate in having a wife who supported me, and put the family first too, or maybe I was born into a generation when this was more common. But the most important role of a wife is to keep your feet on the ground and mine never had any difficulty with that. There is only one chairman in our house, and it is not me. Her only question when I came home and told her we were being asked by Unilever to move someplace else was, 'When do we leave?' She might argue with that and say that at all times she sacrificed her own preferences in favour of following this career path of mine, and I would be the last to suggest that there were not sacrifices she made along the way. All I know is that as we passed through every stage of my career there was a sense of enjoyment, a sense of, 'Gosh, we're glad we're here' or 'Aren't we lucky to be here? Isn't this fun to be doing?' In all those years abroad – we spent 23 of our Unilever years abroad – there was never any sense of 'Isn't it time we left this place? I don't like it, it doesn't suit me.' That was never in her vocabulary. So I have been immensely fortunate.

In many ways Unilever made good provision for expatriation, with decades of experience of doing it. Most of the bases in that regard were properly covered. Appropriate housing was provided in whichever place one lived and worked; there was a full recognition that there were certain commitments and obligations back home that needed to be met if any sort of continuity at home were to be preserved. We were not required to cut off the past when we moved on, and there was a recognition that there were special problems in relation to education for one's children, which in my case meant that we had to send our children to boarding-schools at certain times. This happened to present no conflict with our own sense of what was best for them, and seems to have worked out well. Having said which, I am sure they would all argue that while they gained a lot in areas which other children do not gain, they may have lost in other areas. So one might have certain doubts – more doubts in retrospect than one had at the time.

Inevitably there were important personal occasions when I could not be present. When they were small they were with us. Wherever we were they were, and I threw myself into co-operating as a parent, in their schools' management. I was the chairman of the board of governors at their school in Thailand, for example. And when they went away to boarding school we had annual home leave that was quite generous. So we chose times for being home to fit in to some extent with their holidays and similar sorts of things. But inevitably there were many occasions missed, and people like grandparents stood in for us. You cannot have it all, can you? Those are the balances that are unavoidable.

Those were times in which companies like Unilever were sending out large numbers of expatriates from their home countries – predominantly the UK and Holland, but progressively also from other places as the company sought to move towards a much lower cost and much higher level of effectiveness in world trade, and to high-quality local management. That process took an awful lot of time to accomplish. Consequently, in those years the whole idea was to promote expatriation as a means of Unilever's own particular form of colonisation, if you like, and so it was necessary to put things in place for managers and ensure that things worked smoothly. This was recognised as a corporate requirement. In a company like Centrica, where I now am, where for the first time we have acquired businesses in North America and we are sending people out there, we are having to generate from a standing start a whole bundle of those sorts of services to encourage our people and persuade them to go. People who came into a career in British Gas did not expect to spend huge amounts of time in North America, so this is a new experience for them and for the company. We are having to address those issues. But a Unilever trainee came in expecting a fair chance of going abroad. Of course, a relatively small proportion actually did go abroad, but enough to make it necessary to create special programmes for them.

In Unilever there were people who managed all these things on behalf of expatriates abroad, and the whole management development programme of the company in those years, perhaps still today, involved keeping careful tabs on where certain people were in their career development. One of the key worries for people going abroad was, and I guess still is, the extent to which they get outside the promotional stream in their units back in Europe, and the degree to which the move is seen to be career-damaging or career-enhancing. All sorts of policies described as 'return ticket' arrangements were developed, though they did not always entirely fulfil their objectives. A locally based UK Unilever subsidiary, having sent Joe Bloggs abroad, would solve the problem of his disappearance pretty rapidly. Then he would have to take his chances along with everybody else when new vacancies occurred in the UK. All you could do was insist that when Joe Bloggs was due to come back or had demonstrated potential for promotion, that the company from which he had come should give some priority to his situation over third parties. Sometimes that worked, sometimes it did not. But if you could not demonstrate that sort of care people would be reluctant to go abroad. There was a time, one cannot deny it, when Unilever, in common with many other multinational companies, did not send its best people abroad but sought to solve some of its problems at home by unloading certain people – sending them abroad and then looking aghast when they had to take them back. That also meant you often had the wrong kind of people expatriating. That all changed many years ago but it was an early problem for expatriation. I do not have much basis on which to judge whether Unilever were better about this than other multinationals, except that I now have a son-in-law who works with BP and is following a very similar kind of progression to the one that I followed, and I see that things look pretty much the same. The provisions that I would expect to be in place appear to be in place to his satisfaction.

Unlike some, I never planned a career and said to myself, 'This is what I am going to set my hat at.' One thing always led to another. I am very cautious about young people who appear to be concentrating more on their next job than on their present one. My advice to them always has been: give 100% of your energy and time and thought to what you are doing now and think less about what might happen next. That might be easy for me to say. I came from a company with a thoroughly well-oiled management development system that looked upon career progression as a major source of the preservation of corporate proprietary knowledge, of skills and experience. That is perhaps less the case now but I see the pendulum swinging back again. There was a period in the 1980s when companies rationalised business problems of downsizing, by talking about portable careers and portable pensions. It was a rationalisation of what was actually being forced upon them – massive redundancies and so on – but what got lost in all of that as companies eagerly embraced the opportunity to let people go was that they were getting shot of a huge amount of corporate memory and cumulative experience. It's quite different in companies like this one, Centrica, where one has to go out and hire a great number of people to fill the ranks of a fast-growing business. In so doing you are buying a bit of somebody else's corporate experience, and the development of that uniqueness which determines your own position is much more difficult to establish. In this company we are now looking much harder at the whole question of graduate recruitment, career planning and career development, to find ways of providing the retention motivation to our best people – not just by paying a lot more, but also providing them with the whole raft of satisfactions that I found very motivating in my own career.

I did not do much travelling alone until much later on in my career. During the years when I lived abroad, my job was in the place I was posted to, and the requirement to travel elsewhere was really quite minimal. One or two conferences a year, something like that. They may or may not have been tied into periods of home leave anyway, so the occasions when the family were without me were limited and short in duration. Later on, based back here in the UK, one was seldom out of an aeroplane. But by that time, anchored back into one's home country, the same considerations did not apply. One just got on with it. I think my wife recognised during my time on the Unilever board that those were years that had to be virtually written off as far as the normal pursuit of domestic priorities was concerned.

I looked upon time for relaxation as a major priority. As I mentioned, it is an in-built need, and it was easier in the earlier years than later. But the pace of life in many overseas businesses was rather less hectic than perhaps it is today, so generating leisure time was not hugely difficult. One worked late nights quite frequently, but weekends were relatively undisturbed and that is when one did one's leisure activities. I always also found it desirable to hurl myself into one form of social or community activity or another and we did that as a family too – churches, choirs and that sort of stuff. Anyway I am a bit of a joiner of things like clubs and groups, and I often did that with my wife.

In my overseas posts – and by that I mean our time in Thailand, Argentina and Japan, and Holland to some extent too because we were there for quite a long time – a lot of our friendships were with fellow expatriates in the company, or associates from companies like ours, but we made a large number of local friends in each place too. Working in overseas markets often did put serious strains on marriages, and while strong marriages did not have a problem the opportunities to be led off the path are more available in some places abroad and some people got off the path with considerable glee. Experienced though Unilever was in these issues, there was no counselling for people, not in the modern sense of counselling. Counselling in those days largely meant a swift kick up the arse. It seemed to work quite well. Seriously, people were sent home if they got themselves into great difficulties abroad.

It did not happen much earlier on, but later in my life I quite often had to fly back from holidays for meetings. When major things like acquisitions were running I made sure I could be reached at any moment in time. One needed to be available for instant decision-making. I once had to abort a trip in New Zealand and rush off back to New York, leaving my wife somewhere stranded between Wellington and Auckland. I remember being called back from holidays on the Continent for this or that crisis. There was a little event called Persil Power, which started when I was in my house in France. The first contact I had from Procter & Gamble on that particular occasion was a telephone call from P&G's boss Ed Artz to me in France, which had me scurrying back here quite rapidly. Things like that did not happen very often, but when they did my family realised and accepted that it was important.

What happened much more often was the number of times when it was necessary for business reasons to turn down invitations of a personal nature, invitations one would have like to have fulfilled. In later years that became more of a burden, both to the family and to me. Yes, there were plenty of major occasions when one wished one could have done so-and-so but the company got in the way.

Though I am very competitive, and that never seems to stop no matter how old you get, I have never been a hugely athletic person so I do not have a compulsion to take physical exercise as some people do. I was a moderate golf player and in my younger years I liked to play cricket, and I was a rugby referee and I enjoyed all that. I played some squash and I swam. But it was all pottering here and pottering there. None of it was obsessive. More importantly, I found it vital to keep my brain active at all times, not necessarily on business. So I got stuck into school governance or chambers of commerce or other things concerned with types of societies that require intense focus, but had no stress attached to them other than . . . well, there is nothing more stressful than chairing parish council meetings! Managing those sorts of circumstances can be more tiresome than an office where you can tell someone to belt up if you feel like it. Nonetheless, the full engagement of the mind in things of that kind were, for me, important relaxations.

Without wanting to over-stress the point, it is certainly true that going to church has been helpful. Whatever one means by spiritual issues or spiritual matters, however one expresses that as an individual, it is certainly clear that a church provides a focal point in which deeper things can be given serious time and thought. I cannot say I always came away feeling that a great deal of it was much more than a merely social activity, but for many people – and for me too from time to time – some kind of spiritual comfort was derived and that was for the good. It is still the case I think.

I suspect my wife would take a flipside view of some of the points I have made. She would agree that by and large the family has benefited enormously from the life we have led. The experiences that they have all enjoyed in one way or another have been enriching for them, and have made them what they are. But there has been a price to pay for some of that. My wife gave up her own career. When we married we straight away got sent to Holland, where she could not continue her work as a State Registered Nurse unless she retook all her exams in Dutch. Since she did not want to do that, she turned her hand to becoming a mother, and she would argue being a full-time wife and mother has been her thing in life. She would say there have been sacrifices that have had to be made along the way, particularly later, for this career thing of mine. But I think she would argue that both of us – not just me – were employed by Unilever for 39 years. She made a lot of friends, with close links and involvements.

She followed the interests and activities of the company – I will not say in as much detail as I did – but certainly with a great deal of interest, though I never discussed business problems with her directly. And the lifestyle that went with it she enjoyed to the full. Now she bemoans the fact that her own withdrawal symptoms from Unilever were greater than mine appeared to be. I took a slightly different view from her. In a business like Unilever, you move from context to context within the same company – in a way most other people have to achieve through swapping from one company to another. In that process you get reconciled to the reality that every few years you are required to set aside all that you have done, to walk away from all the relationships that you have made and to hand them over to somebody else. You move on and do something else. And you get used to the pain associated with that. So retiring from Unilever was just the same. I walked out of the door and I never looked back over my shoulder. I just went and did other things. That has been my attitude to life, and hers too most of the time. The question we ask all the time is, 'OK, what's next? – Never mind what was, what's next?' In that sense I think she missed Unilever more than I did.

Nowadays, as I appraise and assess people, I take a great deal of interest in the choices they have made in relation to their own balances in this context and I worry about people who are workaholics in the sense that they give total priority to work as opposed to every other aspect of their lives. I consider that to be a bad judgment. I immediately say, 'This is a person whose judgment I distrust. Therefore I shall distrust and question their judgment in other matters too.' So the way in which people manage these choices for themselves has a bearing for me on the balance I expect they will bring to bear on the decision-making process.

Looking back, I do not think we would want to change anything very much. I hope I speak for both of us on that. I wanted to get on, I wanted to make progress, but I was not consumed with ambition. I cannot possibly suggest that being separated from the children for six or nine months of the year was an undiluted advantage. There were sacrifices made there. But I would say that neither they, nor the relationships we now have, suffered from that. Quite the reverse. They benefited in many ways. Nothing was taken for granted, as it is in some other families, because everything was precious. We are very close. I am not sure whether we would not have been very close anyway. My wife works ceaselessly at family relationships and she is the anchor point. This finds an echo in all my children and their relationships with us, and maybe some of that is related to some of those separations in the past. But if we had lived at home here in England, whether or not we would have sent the children to boarding-school I do not know. Interestingly my daughters, both of whom were at boarding-school, are now sending their own children to the same school they went to.

One of the great pleasures of semi-retirement is that one can accept personal events as top priority and decline some of the business events that are not so necessary. Today I do not have to be in an office for more than two or three days a week, but I make myself available nonetheless on a seven-day-a-week basis to the people and companies with which I am associated. The trade-off is that a phone call that catches me down a hole I am digging in my garden is always preferable to having to traipse back to London for a meeting. I am all set up with computers and an office at home, and I would rather deal with things from there. When I go to France I take my laptop with me and set it up as soon as I arrive. That is fine by the family because although such things interrupt the day, they are not devastating. I have always worked to secure those family goals which seem to me to be paramount. I think I have just about succeeded. **99**

## Keeping Your Balance

- Before joining a multinational organisation explore the likelihood of being sent abroad. If it is high, ensure the provisions they will make will enable the process to work smoothly for both you and your family, on both outward and return journeys.
- Get involved – by becoming a governor, or in whichever way you can – with your children's schools. This will prove your interest in their education – and will be an education for you.
- If you are posted abroad join local clubs and societies and – better still – get your partner to join them with you.

# Chapter 14

## NICOLA HORLICK

Nicola Horlick is chief executive officer of SG Asset Management.
She was formerly with Mercury Asset Management and with
Morgan Grenfell Asset Management.
Nicola Horlick was born in 1960, and educated at Cheltenham Ladies
College, Birkenhead High School GPDST, Phillips Exeter Academy
(USA) and Balliol College, Oxford. She is married and has had two
sons and four daughters, one of whom died in 1998.

**"I**t is very important to have the right balance. People who try both to have a family and at the same time to be work-aholics, and be in the office all the time, are not getting the balance right. People who ring in sick every five minutes because they have to stay at home, because there is this wrong or that wrong, are not getting the balance right either. You have to be honest with yourself and admit to yourself that if you are in either of those situations, things are not working. Otherwise you are going to have serious problems further down the line. It is really important to be true to yourself about whether you are achieving the right balance, because it is only if you are that you can cope.

I have a strict code about what I am prepared to do and what I am not prepared to do. I am not prepared to stay at work until midnight every night, and I am not prepared to turn up for work at five-thirty in the morning. I have always made it very clear to anybody I have ever worked for that it will be on my terms. My terms are that I come to work at around eight o'clock – I have to get my children ready for school – and I leave at twenty to six. I am happy to take work home if necessary, but if you are well organised you can get most things done during the course of the day. A lot of people work very inefficiently. Having a very busy life with lots of children makes you more disciplined, and more efficient.

I have always been completely honest with my employers. I say, 'Take it or leave it, that's how I work.' If they want to leave it, fine. There will be somebody else who is happy to employ me. If people are happy about their working arrangements you get more out of them. If they are constantly in fear of their boss or the organisation or feel that they are being hounded – they suffer from paranoia. And most men would think you were a bad mother if you did not go to the sports day or the carol concert. They recognise the effect that not going would have on a child later in life. You can imagine a major argument at age 18, with your child banging on the table and saying, 'It's because you never came to see me in the carol concert!' You cannot put your children in that position. You have to be there for them. What would an employer rather have? A top-rate woman with children or a second-rate man?

I never, ever, work at weekends. I have five children and I do not have any weekend help, so how could I? At the weekend I am completely tied to the sink and the cooker and the children. There is no way that I could do anything else, and in my view it would anyway be wrong. During the week I have a nanny and we have people to clean and iron and all that sort of stuff. But at the weekend I look after the children, and if we go on holiday I look after the children – with my husband of course – and I do not want other people around. It is very important to me to be looking after them. I very occasionally take business phone calls on holiday. Just once or twice I have come back from holiday because there have been presentations for new business. I work in a beauty parade world, where we do not have any choice about when we do the beauty parade, and once or twice I have come back for the day, just to make a presentation and gone back again. I do not think that is too bad. But anybody who thinks they are completely indispensable is wrong. It is very important for younger people to be given authority to deal with things in your absence. That is how they progress, and it is only through such delegation that you can possibly cope with being as busy as I am.

The companies I have worked for have accepted my approach. I have been very careful to choose bosses who were sympathetic people, who were family-orientated themselves. It is important to choose the right boss if you are a working woman. It is wise to try to assess your potential bosses and work out what attitude they have to all of this. It is important to ask the right questions and it is important to ask people who have worked in that organisation before, because some bosses will give you the marketing spiel about, 'Oh yes, we're terribly keen on people going to sports days', and then when it comes to it they may not be. So it is essential to do your research properly and assess whether it is the right sort of place for you to work. I have only ever had male bosses but they have all been family-orientated. They have been the sort of men who would go to a carol concert or a sports day themselves, not the sort of men who never take any notice of their children. There have frequently been occasions when I have had to miss important business meetings for my children. I would not miss my children's carol concert even for a beauty parade. I just say, 'I am sorry, I can't do that.' My colleagues accept that, and someone else will do it, and the clients accept that perfectly.

You absolutely need the support of your husband. It is not just support in terms of helping to look after children, it is also having a partner who is prepared to allow you to have a high-flying career and is not going to be jealous or find it difficult to take. I am extremely lucky. My husband has always encouraged me, not tried to hinder me in my career progress. There have been moments when I have had doubts about whether I should go on working, because you cannot have a very sick child – as I did for ten years – and not have doubts. But my husband was always a very calming influence, always there to stop me making decisions in the heat of a terrible moment. He would make me take it slowly, think about it and come to a rational decision. And I kept working. It was not a deliberate plan; I just slipped back into work and things seemed to go OK. Everybody seemed to be happy. If I had felt that anybody was suffering in any way – my sick child, my healthy children, my husband – I would not have continued, because in my life they come first.

My husband helps with the practicalities, too. Occasionally I might have to attend something and our nanny might need to go somewhere and I might need to ask my husband to make sure he is at home that evening, and he would have to put the children to bed. It does not happen very often, because I am disciplined about how many things I agree to do in the evenings. I could go out every single night of the week, but I restrict it to two nights a week. Very occasionally, at Christmas and the end of the year, when there are so many things going on it just isn't true, I might be out three nights a week. But even then I will turn things down to ensure that I am at home at least two nights a week. And when I go out I usually go home to put them to bed first – normally I have to change anyway. I see the children, spend some time with them and then go out. It just means they go to bed slightly earlier than they normally would. Sometimes – like last night, when I had to go to the National Theatre because I am on its development council and they had a Gold Members' Evening – I have to go straight out because there just is not time to go home and come back again. But that is extremely rare.

You learn to manage it all as you go along. I have spoken to lots of other people about it, but I am not into reading books about this sort of stuff! I do not read any business books at all. I do not read any self-help books because I do not believe I need that sort of help. That may sound arrogant, but it is mainly to do with time – and I find those sorts of books irritating anyway. I do read novels, but that is escapism, because I sometimes need to escape from the real world.

Having so many children it is very difficult to have any hobbies. The hobbies I have, like skiing, are things that can include the whole family. Apart from that I like going to concerts and I love the theatre. I do not feel under any pressure. I am hyperactive, and I feel unbelievably tired if I have not got anything to do. It makes me really, really tired and I fall asleep instantly. I am obviously an adrenalin junkie.

For ten years I had a very sick child. So for ten years I lived with huge uncertainty, and that taught me that you can never plan things miles in advance. I never knew when my daughter was going to get an infection and would end up in hospital, and that taught me that you need a support system at work in the same way that you need a support system at home. At home I have a nanny and a cleaner and somebody to do the ironing. At work I needed to make sure that if I disappeared for any reason there would be people to pick up the pieces and run with the ball. It was very important to learn that lesson. Really successful people know you need to delegate and they are good at it. They also are self-confident enough to be able to surround themselves with people who are at least as good as they are themselves, and preferably better. They do not suffer the insecurity that means they always surround themselves with people who are not as good as them, who are just 'yes men'.

My sick daughter, Georgie, had a bone marrow transplant and I ended up in Great Ormond Street for a year with her, and so both the support systems had to be working – my home support system and my work support system. That was unbelievably horrific. The work bit was not so bad because I knew there were other people dealing with it – and anyway it was irrelevant in the scheme of things. But the home situation was extremely difficult because I had left four children at home with a nanny, or with my mother, or with someone else. My husband and I took turns to look after them at weekends, in between being in the hospital. That put us under enormous pressure – to the point where it was almost unbearable. Ultimately my daughter died, and then we had to deal with the aftermath of that – our own grief.

I had not realised – I suppose it had never occurred to me – that when somebody that close to you is seriously ill your emotions go up and down together with those of your partner and your children, because your feelings are determined by what you are told by the medics. If they say it is bad news you all feel depressed together. If they say it is good news you all feel happy together. With grieving, you all grieve in different ways and at different times. So you yourself might be feeling a bit better about it one day, but your spouse might be in the depths of depression. In some ways that is a good thing because it means that you can support each other more effectively. My daughter died three years ago next week, so it is not that long ago. Working helps me to deal with it because it keeps me busy. It stops me dwelling on it. If I had not kept busy I would not have been able to deal with it as well as I have. That has been very important.

Achieving a good work/life balance should be easier for men, shouldn't it? They should be disciplined enough not to stay at work unnecessarily. It is more difficult when men have jobs that involve large amounts of travelling. It is not just that they do not see so much of their children, it is much harder to maintain a relationship with your family at all if you do not see them for long periods. But on the whole it should be easier for men. Social convention is such that the woman, even if she works, is still expected to be the primary carer for the children, the person who organises all the childcare, all the washing, all the ironing, all the shopping, all the cooking – everything. That puts an enormous burden on the woman and some women find they cannot manage it, because physically you need to be very strong. You need a huge amount of stamina to be able to do all those things and some women just aren't that strong.

I am not as ambitious as other people suggest I am. I do not think it is ambition that drives me. A lot of it has been to do with having a sick child. It is really a form of escapism. Keeping busy kept me sane and stopped me from being dragged down into the depths of depression. I am a natural optimist so I could not deal with depression. It is not my natural state of mind. I really fear being dragged down by something like that, because I do not know how I would cope with it. I need to keep going, keep looking forward, keep doing something positive. It is the need to be stimulated mentally and the need to have new challenges the whole time that motivates me, not blind ambition. I am not sure women are that ambitious. Ambition is more of a male trait. Women do not trample on anyone on their way to get to the top of the tree. They are more inclusive, which comes from the natural maternal instincts that women have – I am obviously very maternal, otherwise I would not have had six children! And I operate in the office as I do at home. I regard the people here as my family. I try to nurture the young people and bring them through, and I encourage talented people – not stamp on them because they might be a threat.

My friends are very important to me too. My husband and I met at Oxford and a lot of the people we know were at Oxford with us, but there are also people that we have met in the City who quite often, again, were at Oxford – probably at the same time but we just did not know them then. We have met friends through our children too, and that is good because it means you meet people who are in a different industry, whether they are designers or restaurateurs or this, that and the other. I see my friends at lunch-times, and at home in the evenings, and at weekends when we make sure that we always have people to lunch on Sunday. The children like to have other families there, and lots of children to play with, and lots of our friends also have lots of children, four and five children maybe. I hate being alone – which is just as well, isn't it?

I think about issues and problems going to and from work, and when I am going to sleep at night. However busy you are it is amazing how much time there is to reflect. I start to wake up at about six and I lie there between six and quarter to seven thinking about things. Sitting in taxis, sitting in tubes, sitting in aeroplanes, sitting on trains, going to places. If I am going from one business meeting to another in a taxi I am more inclined to be thinking about business. At the weekend when I am driving to get the shopping I am more inclined to be thinking about the children. There is plenty of opportunity to reflect.

Could I be more successful in business if I did not put so much energy into my family? Well, I do not think I have done badly. I am rather surprised that I have done as well as I have. I cannot quite work out how it happened. I have had six lots of maternity leave and I have been in hospitals for long periods of time, yet I still managed to be running a business at the age of 30 and setting up this business at the age of 36, and all through that time I had a very sick child and was having more babies. Luckily I had the stamina to keep going. I also think women are good at thinking about all sorts of things at the same time. As well as my husband I have had a lot of support from my mother, who is young – she is only 62 – and my brother, who lives in London and is always very helpful. If I am stuck he will always do something for me. And I have a good nanny. In total I have had a good support system around me. That has been essential, otherwise I would not have been able to do it.

Like all things in life, there is an element of luck and an element of hard work. I believe in fate and never more so than now, after my daughter dying, because everything possible was done for Georgie. The doctors at Great Ormond Street adored her and they did everything in their power to save her, and I did everything in my power, and my husband did everything in his power. We were all there for her and she knew that and yet she did not survive. One can only say, 'Well, that was preordained. That was always going to happen.' There is no point in carrying on with the 'Why us? Why her?' routine because that is not going to provide you with any answers. That is always how it was going to be. But it leaves me here today without Georgie, with a whole lot of children feeling traumatised, and I just have to get on with things. You have to look forward, and you have to keep going and be determined. It is not so much for personal gratification, or for the money. It is to keep my own state of mind healthy.

I do not think I will ever stop working. I went to a charitable lunch earlier today, where there were a whole lot of people – I would say their average age is probably 70 – and they were people who have been unbelievably successful in life, and as far as they are concerned they are all still working. People like that cannot stop. If they stop they probably just die. There is no point in trying to think that somehow I am going to go and sit in a cottage in Devon with roses round the door and sip tea and stroke the pussy-cat because that is not me. That is not what I am likely to do. I have an 87-year-old grandmother who still visits my uncle in Australia and she goes on several foreign holidays a year – she does not have a huge amount of money so they are very cheap holidays, on coaches or on very cheap flights – but she keeps going and she is a great inspiration to me.

I hate mobile phones. I never leave my mobile phone on. I occasionally turn it on to collect messages but I find mobiles are intrusive. It is rude to have phones ringing every two minutes when you are trying to hold conversations with people. It is wholly unnecessary to speak to people as much as people do. It also could well give you brain cancer. I find mobiles are a real pain in the neck, although they are quite useful if you are stuck on a motorway and your car has broken down. That's about all! E-mail is quick and efficient and very good if you are communicating with people overseas. I can remember writing long letters on that thin airmail paper as a child. I went to school in America for a while and communicating with people in that way is laborious, and if you are very busy like me you do not get round to it. I can touch-type a few lines to somebody, very quickly, and it helps me to keep in touch with friends and relatives who are overseas. Business colleagues do not have my home e-mail address. I certainly do not spend my evenings reading my business e-mails.

I am a very sentimental person and like to think that I am reasonably philanthropic. I spend a lot of time raising money for charity, and I would find it difficult to do a job that I did not feel was of some social benefit. Here we are managing people's pensions, and it is a good thing to make sure people are going to be reasonably well-off in their old age, and not be either a burden on society or poverty-stricken and not be able to have a good quality of life. The fact that people are living longer and staying healthier means there is a greater need to produce good investment returns for pension funds, to make sure older people live in some comfort.

I do not have any religion. I think we do not understand an awful lot of things, that there is clearly something – obviously there is something – but I cannot describe it or understand it. I would rather just accept that I do not understand it. I am very mathematical and logical and the idea of believing in an after-life and so on is not quite me. But things that have happened to me since Georgie has died have convinced me she is there, and that I will see her again one day. It has also convinced me that it is worth being a good person on this earth because you do not know what the next world will hold. I am sure that if you are a good person it will be rewarded. So I do not have traditional faith or go to church. But I believe in something – certainly not an old man sitting on a cloud with a long white beard – but there is something there and the forces of good, hopefully, are more powerful than the forces of evil, and I want to be aligned with the former rather than the latter. **"**

## Keeping Your Balance

- It may sound like work/life balance in reverse, but working hard can – and does – help people cope with terrible moments in their lives. Work can make pain more bearable.
- When you apply for jobs – particularly, but not only, if you are a woman – make sure your prospective employers really mean the politically correct things they say about work/life balance; check out the reality with other employees.
- The other side of that coin is that you should make clear to prospective employers how much time you intend to devote to your children. Far better to clarify the position up-front than to run into serious snags later.

# Chapter 15

## SIR RICHARD BRANSON

Richard Branson is chairman of the Virgin Group of Companies, a venture capital organisation with investments in the travel, retailing, leisure,music, communications and financial services industries. He is president of the British Disabled Water Ski Association, a committee member of Friends of the Earth, a trustee of the Healthcare Foundation, which he founded, of the National Holiday Fund, of the Trevor Jones Trust, of the Paul O'Gorman Foundation and of the London School for the Performing Arts and Technology.
He was born in 1950, educated at Stowe and is married with two children.

**66** A chieving a satisfactory work/life balance depends, above all, on working with the right kind of company. If you are running your own company it will obviously be easier than if you are not, and if it is easier for you, you should try to make it easier for your managers and staff as well. I am a great believer in the philosophy of 'work hard, play hard'. If you can keep yourself physically fit and mentally alert, and have time to relax, then you will perform far better than people who work every minute of the day and never manage to break away from work.

The thing that forced me to really start taking time off was having children. Fortunately I was reasonably successful from quite a young age, so that by the time I had my children, when they went on holiday I could go on holiday with them. I forced myself to find time to spend three months a year away with my kids, travelling the world, and I managed to get to know them really well – perhaps better than a lot of fathers. Hopefully this has meant that they are more level-headed than they might have been, now they are reaching adulthood.

I was also fortunate in managing to find a tiny little island when I was 25, just before having the kids. It was a deserted island and we built a house there, and that is where we retreat. We spend time there with our friends and family and so on. That is where my kids really got brought up, in the holidays. It is run as a business, like everything I do. When I go there I pay rent for it, because I do not feel you should have personal extravagances the company pays for. Anyway one needs to be sure things like that stand on their own two feet, financially. And if you are in the public eye it is quite nice to be able to go somewhere where you can be completely among friends and not feel you are in a goldfish bowl.

We push off when term breaks up. The family knows that when we are there I am going to have to get up early in the mornings and do some work, but I am around, not at an office. Being in the Caribbean, by the time lunch-time comes, phones are beginning to stop ringing, because people are starting to go to sleep in Europe. Then I can spend a lot of time with my family in the afternoons and evenings.

I try never to break into holidays. I had to come back when the decision about the National Lottery was coming through. But generally speaking, I have not broken into holidays. If holiday times are pencilled out of my diary well in advance, people know they are just not going to see me then. Occasionally I might get somebody to fly out to visit me on holiday, but even that happens seldom. There are obviously some reasons for meeting people face-to-face, for certain kinds of deal arrangement, or if you are trying to judge somebody you are taking on, but so much can be done on the phone. You can do lots on the phone.

I read an article the other day that argued it should be against human rights to phone staff at home at weekends and so on. I do occasionally ring staff in the evenings or at weekends. I do not think they mind. I think they would rather hear from me than not hear from me. But if I am abroad I do check what time it is, and try not to wake them up. Generally speaking, they try to do the same for me.

And the wonders of fax machines, e-mails and telephones mean many people can work from almost anywhere. I have always really worked from home. I began to work from a houseboat when I was about 17 years old. Later my children and my wife were living on the houseboat, so kids would be crawling through the office, and nappies would be changed in the office. It was a little bit cramped and perhaps a little bit unfair on my wife – but in those days she would rather have had me around than not around! Then, as the company grew more successful, we managed to buy two houses. The office house was next door to my home. We ended up moving back into one house where I work and the kids, though older, are here as well when they are around.

I generally prefer to have people around rather than not to have people around. At the same time, I often work on my own. There are times when I even find it distracting to have secretaries around. I have four secretaries who work in an office just down the road, but I very rarely have a secretary who actually works with me, because if I have somebody in the same room I just find I have not got time to think – or I feel guilty that I am not giving them something to do.

I do my best to get back home at weekends. I spend 250 days a year travelling overseas, believe it or not, as most of our businesses are overseas now, but I always do my best to be back at weekends. Not every weekend, but as many as possible. And I have done my best to get back from abroad to be at my children's school events. I suppose one of the advantages of owning an airline is that I can get cheap air travel. As long as the airline is making money, anyway.

When I am away I make some of my biggest decisions. If I am lying in a hammock, looking out over the Caribbean, I have lots of time to think. Instead of people bombarding you with things that they want, as they do at the office, you can think about the things you want and the company needs. People at Virgin jokingly say they are more nervous when I am away than when I am here, because it is then that I come up with lots of new ideas.

I do not see business as work. I do not see what I do as work. I see what I do as a way of life, as a challenge. It is a fascinating challenge, trying to change things and create things. In the same way perhaps that an artist enjoys painting, I enjoy creating things, and changing things, and seeing what I am capable of. What I do is so varied, it never gets boring. It is just great fun, fantastic fun.

I was brought up with praise lavished upon me by my parents. Even if I did not deserve it, it made me feel good. I have done the same with my children. Kids know when they have done wrong and they do not need it rammed down their throats. The same applies with people who work for companies. All of us love to be praised and love to feel wanted, so a lot of my time is spent out and about with my staff. When I am on one of our planes I am always on my feet in the aisles, talking to the staff and to the passengers. I always stay in the staff hotels, always go out partying with them. If we are in the Caribbean, and there is a crew nearby in Antigua, we will invite them down to the island.

Getting to know the staff well is important. Even at two in the morning, after a few drinks with them, I have a little notebook in my pocket and I scribble down what I am learning at the bar. I learn more from being in touch and out partying with them than I would behind a desk. And it's fun. It is fun for me, it is fun for them, and it is a damn sight better than sitting in a boring businessman's hotel with no company.

If I invite 18 cabin crew down to the island while I am holidaying, I know they will be fun people, and we'll have a party. It is not a bad existence. My children are of an age where they can enjoy the company as well – and my wife is very understanding and is used to it. Ever since I have known her – we got together 26 years ago – we have always had lots and lots of people around us, and if she wants to retreat, she can retreat. In any event I spend more time with her and the family than most fathers, let alone fathers who are as busy as I am. With my first wife – I was married when I was 19 – I was building the business and I had no children. Trying to build the business from scratch was all-consuming. I had to work 20 hours a day, and that certainly put a strain on the relationship. She is still great friends with Joan and myself – we had dinner with her last night – but when we were married she just gave up on me in the end. We were married only for about three years. I think when you are building a business it is really difficult to get the balance right, because survival is all that matters. You are not going to enjoy your holidays and your time off if you think there is a danger of your company going bust all the time. So 20 hours a day working was the norm in those early days. But once you have climbed over the wall and you have things on a slightly more level keel, then you can get the balance right. I suspect you ought to get the balance right earlier, but it is very difficult to do.

And during the course of the year I still work long hours on weekdays, but I try to make sure I disappear to our cottage in the country at weekends. I do try to do lots of sports at weekends – tennis, hot-air ballooning, cricket, occasional golf – and try to find time for friends. Yes, it can be very, very, long hours on weekdays. But when the children are at school and doing their homework late into the evenings, you are not really going to have valuable time with them. If I go out socially with friends during the week I am so exhausted I am not really giving of my best anyway, so I might as well work really hard on weekdays and then enjoy the holidays and the weekends.

How does my approach ricochet down the company? About six months ago I sent a note out to all our HR people, throughout all the Virgin companies. It said that if people want to go on unpaid leave, we should have a system where they can go on unpaid leave; if people want to work part time, we should introduce systems where they can go part time; if people want flexible working, they should have flexible working; if people want to work four days a week instead of five days a week, we should work out ways of allowing them to do so; and if people want to work at home, we should do our best to make it so they can work at home.

It is a real struggle to get that through. Managing directors and HR departments are set in their ways. Sometimes they come up with good reasons, sometimes they come up with poor reasons. But at Virgin Atlantic, if our flying crews want to go on unpaid leave they can, and so many volunteer to do so that we have ended up taking on about 300 to 400 extra people, to cover the crew members who are taking unpaid leave. That means 300 or 400 extra jobs have been created on a permanent basis.

If every company did that there would be far fewer people unemployed in the country. And the people who were employed would be doing jobs that were tailored to their needs. Mothers would have more time for their children. Fathers would have more time for their children. Parents who did not need to both work full time could have one person working full time and one person working 50% of the time. One must aim at trying to get the right balance in all this. Saying everybody should work four days a week, or that nobody can work more than 35 hours a week, is taking things to extremes. Some people want to work 60 hours a week; others want to work 30 hours a week. It is up to employers to try to achieve that ideal situation, and I think it is for government to encourage it. At Virgin it is up to me to make sure people are able to feel they have the right balance, and we still have a long way to go to achieve that. The country as a whole has got a long way to go. We have to be much more adventurous.

We have 50,000 people who work for Virgin. So, how much time should one spend on one's own two children, and how much time should one spend on the 50,000 people? Obviously they are all important, so it is an important balancing act. But all the other people have got their own families, so you have to make sure you are a good father to your own children. For example, my son has just turned 16 and I went away with him on a boat for six days, just the two of us.

My wife and I are fortunate in that we are opposites. Joan is a Glaswegian who is not really interested in business. We were away last weekend and my telephone battery had gone wrong, so I swapped phones with her and was just about to put her SIM card into my phone when she said, 'There's no need for that, because Holly and Sam are with us. So I don't need the phone.' She is a mother whose principal interest is the kids and as long as everything is well with them that is her main concern. At the same time, she has been a fantastic person to lean on. But I do not really discuss business at home too much. Joan is understanding, but strong-willed. She says what she thinks, is extremely down-to-earth, has no pretensions. We obviously lead a good life, but she is not interested in jewellery or expensive cars or anything like that. She has her priorities right basically, and her main priority is to make sure that we find the time for the kids.

Some of all this goes back to the way I was brought up. I was very fortunate in having a happy upbringing with parents who were happy together and I am determined to pass that on to my own children. It has worked out that way, and we are still as happy together as we were 26 years ago. That gives enormous stability to me in my working life too.

I think it extremely important that you 100% believe in what you are doing, or there is no point in doing it. Unless you feel you are going to make a difference and that you are going to change the world in some small way in whatever field you are in, then there is no point in bothering. That applies throughout our company. It is critical that people who work in our train division know that they are going to make a difference, they are going to transform the rail network in this country, and that people who work in our planes know that they are offering the best service in the air. People in the financial services company, hopefully, believe that the financial services industry will never be the same again because Virgin has gone into it. One has got to make a difference. We use the money that we make from these companies to reinvest in more companies, or we may try to use some of it to tackle internal social issues. I think a company needs a mixture of both, if for no other reason than the morale of the staff will benefit from it.

I stumbled into being an entrepreneur. Originally I just wanted to be an editor. In order to be an editor, I soon found that I had to become an entrepreneur to keep my magazine going. Ever since then I have generally gone into things where I have found that I have been frustrated. Flying on other people's airlines, I did not like the experience. I thought things were being done pretty abysmally, and felt I could go in and make a difference and do better. Almost every single business we have gone into has started from that premise. I get my satisfaction from people saying, 'I've just come back on Virgin Atlantic and it's the best airline I have ever flown on'; or 'I have just been on your new cross-country train, and what a difference'; or 'I have just been into one of your new health clubs and it's transformed my life'; or 'Thank you, your helicopter ambulance in London has just saved my daughter, and we'll forever buy your music!' – or whatever.

I was brought up on general moral premises, such as love one's neighbour, try to be unselfish and so on. If I said something unpleasant about somebody my mother would straight away say, 'That just reflects on you and I don't want to hear you say that ever again.' It was a good, basic, moral upbringing. I have not always stood by those premises perfectly, but I go to sleep feeling that what I have done during the daytime is something I can be proud of, and never go to sleep feeling guilty. Being able to sleep well at night is quite a good way of judging whether one is leading a good life or not. One day you are going to have that last night before you go to sleep permanently, and it will quite nice to know that you have managed to tick everything off in a fairly decent manner.

Every year I take my father and all our family and friends away for his birthday, and he is now 85. When I went ballooning or boating, I would take my parents with me to Japan, to Morocco, to South Africa or wherever the balloons or boats where heading from, so I managed to spend a lot of time with them. Just before she died my grandmother wrote to me saying the last ten years of her life were the happiest of her life, and she was well into her nineties. As a family we have managed to stay close right across generations and that has been fantastically valuable. **99**

## Keeping Your Balance

- Spend as much time as you can, while you can, with your parents.
- Getting away alone for a few days with children is a great way of getting to know them.
- Before phoning from abroad check the time at home.

# Chapter 16

## LORD STEVENSON, CBE

Dennis Stevenson is chairman of HBOS, of Pearson, of Aldeburgh Productions and of the House of Lords Appointments Commission. He is a director of the Economist Group, of Manpower and of Glyndebourne Productions and a member of the British Council. He was formerly chairman of the SRU Group, of Intermediate Technology Development Group, of AerFi Group, of Aycliffe and Peterlee Corporation and of the Tate Gallery, and a director of London Docklands Development Corporation, Tyne Tees TV, Thames Television, J Rothschild Assurance, BSB Group, and Lazard Brothers. He is a special advisor to the Prime Minister and the Secretary of State for Education, a governor of the London School of Economics and of the London Business School and a member of the Panel on Takeovers and Mergers.

Dennis Stevenson was born in 1945 and was educated at Glenalmond College and King's College, Cambridge. He is married and has four sons.

**"I** think myself very lucky to be alive now, and to be in the position I am in. It is possible for me to achieve a balance between personal and work life that was not possible for my father. This is partly because a number of developments at work have made it easier to combine a very engaging and full work life with being involved in the lives of your wife and your children, and partly – something that is often underrated – because of the other side of what I would loosely call 'feminism': the fact that women have allowed their husbands to be more concerned with domestic activities and with the children. My father, who adored his children, probably never changed a nappy. That was not because of a dis-inclination on his part but because of the social mores of the time – and those mores have changed.

More generally, if I put on my hat as corporate old fart and chairman of two of the country's very largest companies, I would strongly like everyone working for me and with me to be able to achieve a balance between their personal and work lives, and it is increasingly possible. Today it behoves employers to create an atmosphere and an environment which says both 'We do not care when you do your work so long as you get it done', and 'We would rather employ rounded human beings who have a private life and a private infrastructure than obsessional little twits.'

Big corporations are much more understanding than they were. But then a number of things have happened to make it easier for them to be understanding, quite aside from developments in social attitudes, enlightenment and progressiveness. First, technology has changed the nature of production processes – fewer large corpora-tions need thousands of people to be doing exactly the same thing at exactly the same time with exactly the same machine tools; work is much more easily taken home. Second, technology makes it easier to work from home, in that you can use e-mail from home; you can conference-telephone from home, the price of video conferencing from home is falling dramatically; and the mobile telephone means you can be watching your little darling play football and talk to California at the same time. (I would thoroughly disapprove of anyone doing that, but they could go to a corner of the football pitch and do it out of other people's hearing!) So as corporations have become more progressive they have been aided and abetted by technological developments.

If you are unlucky enough to have a job where your colleagues depend upon you being there between eight-thirty and five-thirty, five days a week, and if when you are not there you are letting everyone down, then that is a tough position to be in. But if you are not in that position, and increasingly people are not, you should be using your creativity and imagination to try to find ways of combining home with work. In the two companies of which I am chairman – Pearson and HBOS – many people are in that happy position. In both companies there are loads of workaholic-type jobs that require you to work 60, 70 hours a week, but in very many of them you can choose exactly when and where you work those hours. It is easier in Pearson than in HBOS. In HBOS, with its retail branches and call centres, it is much less easy. There are far more people who work in shifts. But I hope we at HBOS are becoming more and more flexible about when people work shifts, how they work shifts and so on. So within the constraints of the business, I press everyone working in my companies to achieve a good balance. I constantly talk to them about it and encourage it.

For the companies this is partly enlightened self-interest, but I would not rest my case on the fact that having well-rounded employees leads to superior shareholder returns. Nice guys don't always win. Undoubtedly there are lots of very successful corporations driven by fear, with obsessional twits – or shits – at the top. I rest my case on an enlightened view of how human beings should treat each other, rather than on producing great returns for shareholders. Speaking for myself, I like working in an atmosphere where people feel they are being treated properly, and are themselves treating other people properly. If you want to make a bigger case for the well-balanced life, it is an aspect of capitalism. Capitalism gives more people more freedom to make their choices. Capitalism is the least bad way of creating wealthy human beings.

It is clearly harder for women working full time than for men, but we are beginning to see the first signs of something that is long overdue: families where the woman is the hunter-gatherer and the man is the domesticated partner. Corporations should be using their corporate ingenuity to employ new technologies to make it easier and easier for women, and for men, to combine responsibilities towards families and children with responsibilities to work. That is certainly in corporations' enlightened self-interest.

If you have a very able 30-year-old woman working for you who is going to have three children over the next six or eight years it is in your corporate interest to keep her engaged in the operation. But anyway it is the right thing to do. For a small investment, corporations can put all the right kit into women's homes, so that when they go away on maternity leave the presumption is not that they are off the air for three to six months. The presumption is that they may be on the air every day, or they may not be on the air but they can follow the business at home, because they can get everything downloaded in real time. They can keep up with what is happening there. They can communicate with their work colleagues there. A successful and ambitious woman aged 30 who is having a child does not necessarily want to be left to coo with her child and do nothing else for five or six months. She wants to have instant access to the child, but also be able to keep her hand in. A smallish operation that the Halifax acquired recently does all that. It is absolutely terrific. That is what we should all be doing, and I think more of us are doing it.

I realised at an early age I would rather lead the mad hectic work life I lead, and work a huge number of hours rather than do 35 hours at a routine job at a workbench or in McDonald's every day of the week. There is work and there is work. When I read articles about tycoons boasting 'Here I am. I work all those hours . . .' I think, bullshit. A lot of work is hugely satisfying. By and large, mine is. So I will typically get up at six to six-thirty and work at home for an hour or two, come into my office which is – because I am very privileged – conveniently near my home, and I will work on from then until six or seven o'clock in the evening. Then I go home and probably do an hour's work before going to sleep. Or I will nip home for an hour or two and then go out to do something that will probably be work-related, but will also probably involve a delicious dinner. So I could say that most days of the week I work from six-thirty until eleven p.m. – and that would not be a lie – and that some days it is three or four hours less. And at weekends I do a few hours work each day and occasionally more than that. It adds up to a huge number of hours each week.

Nonetheless I have missed a very low percentage of all the sports matches my children have played in – they are all sports mad. I certainly have not missed more than one in five of their matches. Naturally it is jolly helpful to be the boss. This Saturday I am due to go to Paris to attend a business dinner – I will be on duty, making a speech and all that stuff – and my son is playing football for his school in the morning and my wife has something she is doing in the morning, so we will rush to get the two o'clock Eurostar to Paris and we will change on the train – the Paris dinner is black tie – and we will arrive in Paris by eight o'clock. That kind of consideration dominates my life. I have only once missed a teachers' evening and that was because I was ill, not because of work. So I work very hard, very long hours, but each week there must be up to ten hours when I am doing things that are family-connected, during working hours.

From a parent's point of view the school secretary is probably the most important member of school staff, and most parents never know who the school secretary is. The school secretary is the person to oil up to, because if you can get hold of the school calendar and plan the term – ideally ahead of time, when it is in draft – you give yourself an extra three weeks of knowing when things are going to happen. It gives you a huge advantage. School secretaries do not normally let parents see it, but you can get it if you try. Even if you cannot persuade the school secretary, on the first day of term you can get it off your children. As soon as I have it I take out of it everything – every sporting date, every musical date, every meeting of the parents with the teachers and the other kinds of parental event, or lectures at the school. If I know now that in eight weeks' time I am due to have a business dinner and there is a meeting with the teachers the same evening, there is no problem at all in getting out of the dinner. If I am due to have dinner on Tuesday and I learn about the teachers' meeting on Monday morning, it is a tad more embarrassing. But I would still cancel the dinner.

I am completely ruthless about getting out of business things. Though it is a cliché, your children grow up and then they have gone. I feel the same about my wife. It is easy to get into a rut where you do not see much of your wife, or you are so bloody tired when you see her you get snappy. Not that you can always get things right. Nobody can. This Sunday, when I have to be in Paris, it is my youngest son's birthday. Normally on family birthdays we have a ritual where presents get given out around my and my wife's bed in the morning – before I go to work if it is a working day. But we will not be there on Sunday. So I talked to my son and he said, 'Fine.' As the children have got older I have always tried to talk about such difficulties with them ahead of time – and they always say, 'Fine. Don't worry at all.'

My third son suffers from epilepsy, and he is at Cambridge University. If he rang me up and said he was in trouble I would go straight up to Cambridge like greased lightening. I would stop whatever I was doing immediately. On the other hand I had an aunt living in Edinburgh I was devoted to who died last year aged 102. I had a very special relationship with her. For the last 20 years I used to go and see her once every three weeks or so. And over the years she was ill quite often and I would tend to her. If she were alive now and I heard she were ill I probably would not say to you, 'Terribly sorry, I've got to go.' I would check what is happening during the rest of the day, and try not to let anyone down, see who is cancellable, get everything done that was not cancellable, and then go up to Scotland. I would be appalled if anyone working for us did anything different. After 11 September, Pearson's chief executive Marjorie Scardino sent an e-mail to everyone working for Pearson saying that no one needed to go to any meeting or do anything they did not want to. They needed time to sort their minds out. She was as astonished as I was that journalists thought this to be worth reporting, as though she was an amazingly progressive employer. It was terribly obvious: both the right thing to do and hugely motivating – and most people, being responsible human beings, probably worked harder so as not to take advantage of it.

When I myself was more of an obsessional little twit than I hope I am today – when I was young and ambitious, in my twenties – I did not believe in holidays. Then my wife sorted me out. We went through a period of saying, 'What you do is you clear two weeks, you shut the door tight, you have nothing to do with work and off you go.' We did that for a period of about 15 years. Then I realised that if you are responsible for quite complex and unpredictable businesses, it is much better to take a lot of holiday but to be available. When I am skiing – which I do a lot of and which is itself occupational therapy – each evening there will be a set of e-mails waiting and in the morning, by the time I get back on the slopes, I will have dealt with them. So I no longer believe in not being bothered when I am on holiday. Fortunately in the last few years I have not had horrible, stomach-knotting types of holiday interruptions, so it has been OK.

Every day of my life I fill out a sheet on my pad. I put 'ring', 'think', 'dictate', 'do' – and there will be subcategories of 'think', and 'do', and under 'ring' there will be people I have to ring up now, people I will ring this evening and so on. There will be business things and personal things. There are things I need to have thought through today, others that I am probably going to leave till the weekend. It is a very simple system. I tried all the clever trendy stuff, doing it electronically and having special sheets printed and so on, but a piece of paper and a pencil are still the most flexible pieces of technology around. Like everyone else, I tend to duck away from things that are really difficult to think about. But in the end I force myself. At the moment I have got to get my mind around the whole issue of the House of Lords reform because I am involved in it in several different ways. It has been on my think list for the last three weekends. And the pressure is welling up to do something about it. It keeps appearing on my daily sheets.

I certainly could not do what I do without my wife's support. Some of my jobs have involved lots of entertaining, and at an operational level my wife is brilliant at that. When I was chairman of the Tate Gallery for ten years we opened three new museums, which involved endless entertaining, thoughtful entertaining, and my wife coped with all that. But her help has been much more fundamental. When our oldest son was about one year old she read me the riot act. I was four years out of university and over-excited by my own achievements. I had set up my own business, things were going well, and I thought it was clever to work until two in the morning every night. One day she took me apart. She is not the kind of person who takes people apart – she only shouts about once every 20 years while I do so three times a week. She did not threaten to walk out, because that is not her style. She would broadly say, 'Well, you're that kind of a personality – insecurity-driven – and that is fine. If that is what makes you happy, terrific.' She sees that what I do follows on from my personality – and she is very happy not to be like that herself. So she simultaneously encourages me and reins me in. I am very fortunate in being married to someone who has very clear views on these issues – views which, once she had laid down the law, I was very happy to take on board and run with. But she owns the copyright. I am a reasonably organised sort of chap – so having been given my road, I have been very happy to make the journey.

That is why I like to discuss business problems with her. She has a completely different perspective. I used to be really bad at talking about my work, and I had to force myself. I used to come home – perhaps I was under pressure or perhaps it was a male macho thing – and I did not want to admit to her that the issues I needed to discuss were the ones that were worrying me because I thought I was screwing them up, failing. Maybe deep down one does not want to admit that to one's wife. I could not spit it out. That was despite the evidence that on the rare occasions when I did so – I am going back here to when I was in my twenties or thirties – having done so made things much better. I am quite good at all that now. But it has been hard work getting there.

There are people who externalise stress and pressure and are very open about it, and people who do not. I am under huge stress all the time, and one has to be a bit careful. It is a fact of life that the more successful people you look at, the higher the incidence of mental ill health, and the higher the incidence of depression – I mean clinical depression as opposed to just being unhappy. I believe that a high percentage of ministers in all postwar cabinets have suffered from depression. Among the chairmen and chief executives of the top 100 companies right now there are several I could name who suffer from depression. I myself had a bout of clinical depression some years ago although everything was going brilliantly for me at the time – it was short-lived, I am glad to say. So you have to be a bit careful, and realise that if you are working very hard in a lot of different areas, and you have a certain kind of personality, it can do funny things to you. People who lead multivariate lives, as I do, have to externalise their stress even if it means yelling at people or whatever. They handle stress better as a result. People who do not look as though they have much on, who do not show any emotion, are often internally screwed up. In general I no longer feel ground down by stress. I can go home and think, 'I don't like what's happening to this business' or 'I am under pressure', and then I feel sick about it, and miserable about it, but I tend to externalise and let it hang out, and then I feel reasonably relaxed about it. When I am like that my family take the piss. They understand me very well, and they will say, 'Oh God, he's off again!' They understand, but I do not think they are very understanding. They are not very impressed, and they are quite intolerant of me. Rightly so. And if something has gone wrong suddenly, on the spur of the moment, I will try and blame it on one of my secretaries who, I hasten to add, I have worked with for a very long time. They know me too!

One of the things our generation does not talk about is that you can make the conscious choice of saying, 'When I look back on my life, I want to feel I did good in terms of what it was doing. So I worked in a business that produced food well or services well or helped other human beings, rather than in a parasitical business. And I wished to work for a business that tried to treat people properly.' It is essential to believe that what you are doing is worthwhile – though that was never part of my education. I was left-wing, as everyone I knew was, and regarded mammon as wicked. My views were pretty unsophisticated. I did not have any ideas as to alternatives. No one had ever said that in looking at your career choice you might want to do something or make something that will do society good, irrespective of who shares the profits from it. That is a terribly obvious concept but no one ever said it to me. And I am not aware of it cropping up much in my children's education, or that of their peers. But it matters hugely to me.

For example, HBOS is pursuing a radical contrary strategy in the financial marketplace. It is born of the conviction of the chief executive James Crosby that some of the widespread criticism of the banks is correct – and that while it may not be illegal to make money out of large balances in the current accounts of old ladies, and it may not be illegal to have multi-pricing in mortgages, it sure does not pass the conscience test. A few years ago, when people's trust in banks was falling, we took a decision to make our pricing transparent. I am proud of the fact we took something like £500 million off our profits at a time when our share price was on its back, and we said, 'This is the right strategy, a growth strategy.' We removed double-pricing on mortgages. We started paying money on current accounts. That might sound soppy and moralistic to some, but it is our strong view – and by the way, we are going to make money out of it. It was driven by – well, someone at the time said it was an unrealistic, idealistic view of life, but I do not think so at all – it was driven by a view that says, 'We should not be a part of an oligopoly using inertia and obfuscation to prevent you moving your account. We have products and services that will make your financial life better, and if no one else is clever enough to develop them you should pay us high margin and make us a lot of money.'

I am not a great loner, but it is extraordinary that if – this is one of the great secrets in life – you get your children out of the way when you are young enough to enjoy it, you can spend time alone or with your wife, and it is wonderful. I now spend a lot of time alone with my wife. I like shopping. I am interested in paintings. We spend a lot of time gallery-hopping – not just in London but wherever we are. We spend vegetable-like days just wandering around. And I am very into music. I play the violin, and will do so more. So I spend some time on my own, and a great deal of time alone with my wife. My sons do not want to spend that much time with me anyway. They prefer girls.

The really intrusive thing is the telephone. I have a mobile telephone fixed in the car, plus a proper mobile telephone which virtually no one has the number of – my family have it and my secretaries have it and on very rare occasions they might use it to ring me up. I could not even tell you its number, because I use it so seldom. That is deliberate because mobiles are dreadful things – though the wonderful call-minder devices mean you do not have to answer them until you are ready. But my children love their mobiles. They and their friends use them all the time. E-mailing has the potential for intrusiveness, which has not happened to me yet. Marjorie Scardino has terrible problems with e-mail – hundreds and thousands of people send her e-mails and she feels she ought to reply to them. When that happens you have to manage it, and send thousands back automatically saying, 'I can't go on like this' or whatever. I have my own personal e-mail address which, like the mobile number, not many business people know. When I am travelling, my secretaries forward messages to me that way, which is absolutely fantastic. When I was a student I taught myself ten-finger typing, but I almost never use it and I am not very fast. The modern fashion for chief executives to do their own e-mailing is nuts. It is grown men playing with Meccano.

And e-mail is brilliant for keeping in touch with the children. This morning Charles, my son with epilepsy in Cambridge, forwarded to me an extraordinary e-mail. He had written to a don saying he was going to be late with an essay because he'd had a fit, and the don had written back, 'I absolutely understand because I have a son of the same age who has very severe epilepsy.' Then they both entered into an interesting correspondence which ended up with the don talking about epilepsy being a Cinderella. My son then sent me his e-mail saying, 'What did he mean by Cinderella?' I spent fifteen minutes thinking about it, and then remembered that Graham Greene – did you know Graham Greene had epilepsy? – made the great remark that cancer, leprosy and epilepsy were discreet, unfashionable, stigmatised diseases and now in this country we raise around £300 million for cancer, £10 million for leprosy but still only £2 million for epilepsy: epilepsy is the Cinderella illness. So I explained to my son I thought that was what the don meant. Without e-mail all that would not have happened. You can do it any time, any hour of the day. I do not know how people used to survive with their children being out of communication for long periods when they went travelling.

Paradoxically e-mailing has revived the art of letter-writing. There was a time, maybe 80 or 100 years ago, when people wrote personal letters to each other. And then, with telephones, it stopped. E-mails have brought it back. My oldest son pointed out that what he and I are doing, his great-great-grandfather did. Whereas I did not. I wrote business letters but I did not sit down and write, 'My dear so-and-so . . .' which is what our grandparents did, and my son now does with all his friends. They use e-mail instead of the telephone.

There is no question but that I am ambitious, but not calculatingly ambitious. My career was wholly unplanned. Things just happened to me. I was going to be an academic. I thought I was pretty clever and everyone else thought I was clever. Economics is like maths, you know when you are good at it, but I got a lower second in my final exams, which I still do not understand. (Perhaps someone called Stevens or Stephenson got a very pleasant surprise!) That is why I set up a business. I never thought of myself as a businessman. And a series of flukes have happened since. So I have not sat down and said, 'I would like to run Pearson or the Halifax.' I have not done that, or anything like it, but when Richard Rogers rang me and said, 'We would like you to be chairman of the Tate if the Prime Minister could be persuaded' – there was a difficulty because it was well known that I was not Margaret Thatcher's favourite person, as I disagreed with much of what she was doing – 'Would you do it?' it took me three seconds to say, 'Yes.' I had no grounds on which to say 'Yes'. I had never done anything like that before and had no relevant experience but I thought, 'Wow! Yes! Go for it.' So I like exercising power and doing things, hopefully, quite well.

It was because I did not do well in my final exams that I got catapulted into this plural, portfolio life. I had not gone into the Foreign Office, I was not going to do a PhD, I had not gone on a milk round for jobs, so one thing led to another and I found myself the longest-running portfolio job person in Britain. I have been doing it since I was 22. I am running two of our biggest companies, I am doing my job in the House of Lords, I am still doing a lot for the Tate, I am doing this, that and the other – and in a way that I cannot quite rationalise it gives me flexibility and makes it easier to do even more things. It is also a lot of fun. And it makes it much easier to get the work/life balance right. It was a complete fluke that I adopted the plural life and my parents were very worried about me – but it is growing more and more possible for our children to be pluralised. My oldest son is already.

There are two kinds of people in this life. People who have the view, which I personally think is the right one, that once you have sufficient money and are reasonably confident you will be able to have a nice time, making still more money really does not matter.

Then there are people, who I feel very sorry for, who feel that the more they have the more they want. That is a desperate situation to be in. I am very much in the former camp and I just pray that none of my children are in the latter camp. Contrary to what is widely believed, I think loads of people are in the former camp. They might not rationalise it the same way, but most of my friends say they need to have enough money to cover themselves if everything goes wrong, enough money if anyone in their family gets seriously ill, to buy whatever medical help they need, to buy the things they want to buy and to make sure they are not completely destitute in their old age – and that is it, that is fine.

I do spend some time thinking about – spiritual is too grand a word – but anyway, meaning-of-life-type issues, and I constantly reproach myself for not spending more time doing so. I am not religious. I am an agnostic, but if at the end of the day there were a pearly gate and I had to justify myself to someone, I would love to be able to justify myself by going back to first principles. So I do spend some of my time thinking about why we are here and what is right and what is wrong – but not enough, never enough.

Marjorie Scardino and I were at a meeting one morning and at about twelve-thirty I said, 'I am afraid I've got to go.' I am sure she thought I was going to some terribly important meeting. The fact was that I was going to the astroturf pitch at Battersea to watch my son play for his school. It was a grey, cold, drizzly London day sometime in November. I was standing there with various other parents, and then I noticed this bloke and thought, 'What the hell is Marjorie's driver doing here?'

Then I looked again, and there was Marjorie. Her son was playing for the other side. She had thought, 'Yippee. Dennis is off, I can sneak away.'

So you had the chairman and the chief executive of Pearson, on a Tuesday, playing hookey, watching their children play football. I tell that story often in Pearson. And I always add that if you are doing a job where you will be letting everyone down if you are not there, then you cannot mess around. But I am sure Marjorie and I worked until the middle of the night that night. Getting the balance right is what we both aim to do. **99**

## Keeping Your Balance

- Get the school calendar of events as far in advance as possible, enter all the relevant dates in your diary pronto and adjust your business schedule to accommodate them.
- If you make work-lists for yourself (often called 'to do' lists) include personal, family decisions and actions as well as business decisions and actions.
- While on maternity or paternity leave, keep in touch with what is going on at work by e-mail, so you can easily pick up the reins again if and when you decide to return.
- Do not be too proud, too macho, or too scared to discuss your failures as well as your successes with your partner. A problem shared is a problem punctured.

# SUMMARY: BEATING THE 24/7

Nobody works 24 hours a day, seven days a week. Virtually nobody is even on call 24 hours a day, seven days a week. 'The 24/7 life' has entered our colloquial vocabulary as a shorthand way to describe people who work excessively long hours and are almost permanently on call when they are not at work. With a little poetic licence its meaning has been stretched to describe people who seem never to stop working, never to stop thinking about their work, never to stop talking about their work and worrying themselves sick – sometimes literally sick – about their work; people who consequently devote far too little time and attention to their families and their personal lives. In today's society such people – I've called them the millstone managers – are not that rare. As the European Labour Force Survey showed, some 2.2 million managers in the UK work overlong hours. Nobody knows how many managers feel permanently collared by their employers, tethered to their jobs by electronic and psychological leashes, night and day. They can run, but they cannot hide.

'24/7' is literally, of course, a definition of time. 'Time is the scarcest resource and unless it can be managed nothing else can be changed', observed the management guru Professor Peter Drucker. Throughout the 16 interviews with the business leaders, you cannot fail to have been constantly aware of their intuitive acceptance of this dictum. One of the personal qualities that sets highly successful business people apart is their instinctive sense of time as a scarce resource. Many of the interviewees recognise that there have been occasions, particularly when travelling abroad, when they have been unable to control the management of their time as totally as they might have wished. But mostly – often prodded by their partners – they have learned how to organise and balance their time to ensure that non-work activities get an acceptable share of 'the scarcest resource' in their lives.

Right at the start Richard Sykes – hardly an idler! – points out that 'people who work 18 hours a day are mad'. In the next chapter Dominic Cadbury says, 'I was always very conscious that work should not invade my private life to the point where it was going to mean my private life became undermined or prejudiced.' This may be a predictable sentiment from someone brought up in the Cadbury tradition, but it is worth remembering that for well over a century the Cadbury tradition has had two strong and entwined strands: enduring business success entwined with caring passionately about work/life balance issues. Richard Branson – world-famous for combining his hobbies and passions with his business life – says, 'If you can keep yourself physically fit and mentally alert, and have time to relax, then you will perform far better than people who work every minute of the day and never manage to break away from work.' And Michael Grade echoes the same thought when he says: 'You have to take time and make time – you absolutely have to' (having, like Richard Branson, learned the cost of not doing so when he was younger). Rosalyn Wilton, who like several of the others spent an enormous amount of time travelling during her early career, once flew back from Australia to attend a parents' evening. Michael Perry says, 'In my case there is a sort of built-in, almost physiological requirement to create space and create some sort of balance as compensation for periods of pressure.' And so it goes on.

Nicola Horlick insists, 'I have a strict code about what I am prepared to do and what I am not prepared to do.' John Clare agrees, 'In my mind there have always been rules and guidelines to which I have tried to work.' Dennis Stevenson rounds off the 16 interviews with his delightful anecdote about accidentally finding himself with Pearson's chief executive Marjorie Scardino at a soccer match in which their sons are on opposing sides, which reveals the attitudes of both of them to the importance of their families.

The underlying difficulty for all managers is that achieving a good work/life balance is not a one-sided problem. Like most managers, most of the time, the interviewees enjoy their work immensely. In the Institute of Management 2001 study, more than two-thirds of the respondents who expressed a view claimed that 'the stimulation and interest I get from work is more important to me than the financial rewards' – though they did not deny the financial rewards were crucial too. So work and family do genuinely compete for their time. Most managers want to have their cake and eat it: they want both the bun and the ha'penny. That is why there is no such thing as a perfect work/life balance. Several of the interviewees admit they have been through periods of intense work-related stress, but those periods have been dwarfed by the satisfactions they obtain, and have always obtained, from their jobs. Sometimes you have to read between the lines to see it, sometimes they say so overtly.

Dennis Stevenson says, 'A lot of work is hugely satisfying.' John Clare says, 'This business gets into your bones and your blood . . . If you like it, you love it. There is nothing else quite as attractive, exhilarating and stimulating.' Richard Branson says, 'It is a fascinating challenge, trying to change things and create things. In the same way perhaps that an artist enjoys painting, I enjoy creating things, and changing things, and seeing what I am capable of. What I do is so varied, it never gets boring. It is just great fun, fantastic fun.' Rosalyn Wilton concurs, 'I like the challenge of business. I like to do things against the odds – to knock down a few barriers. It is great selling to someone who says they absolutely will not do any business with you.' 'Do I want to change my life?' asks Helen Alexander rhetorically, and answers herself, 'If I did, then I would. And I am not doing so right now.' Clive Hollick makes the point most emphatically:

> You are swept along by it. You are excited by it. Many of us . . . have jobs that we are passionate about and become very engaged in . . . you are really enjoying your work, you really want to go for it, and you are building something and travelling and doing deals and coming up with exciting new ideas and working with a great team of people. It is very heady and you are totally absorbed by it.

'But', he immediately adds, 'the price you pay is that it can push the rest of your life right to the margin.' If you let it, that is. Christopher Bland sums things up when he states, 'In the end you have to plan to achieve your own balance. It will not occur by happenstance. You learn how to do it for yourself. Nobody really teaches you.'

Although nobody really teaches you, all 16 business leaders have individually and collectively provided some principles and some stratagems that can help you to get the balance right. Some of the 'Keeping Your Balance' points at the end of each interview may to you seem obvious, but they may not be so obvious to others; this is an area where people often make the most basic mistakes. Some you may already know, but frequently forget, in which case the lists may help jog your memory. Some may seem impossible for you to achieve at the present stage in your career, but the interviewees stress how much circumstances change over the years, and things that are impossible today may be easily achievable in a year or two. Some of the points, as mentioned earlier, may contradict each other, but different people solve their work/life balance problems in different ways, and only you yourself can decide which is best for you.

For ease of reference I will now reprise the pivotal principles from the opening chapter, followed by the 50-plus 'Keeping Your Balance' points from the end of each interview, slightly abbreviated in most cases and loosely grouped into sections.

## The Pivotal Principles

- Work for organisations sympathetic to work/life issues.
- Calculate your Work/Life Ratio and aim for at least a 50%/50% equilibrium.
- If you are a man, do not ignore your wife's yellow card when your work is fouling up your family's life.
- If you are a woman, make sure your partner will whole-heartedly support your business ambitions, and not be envious of your success.
- Minimise holiday and weekend interruptions, but do not fight them: you won't win.
- Get a private e-mail address and mobile number, and use them to keep in touch with your family.

- Delegation is as important to your personal life as it is to your business life: trust your colleagues.
- At times of real family crisis tell your boss and your workmates what is happening, then scram.
- Important though work and family are, make time for other leisure commitments – these become more important as you grow older.
- If you work in a job you feel to be worthwhile, work/life balance problems will wither and be less irksome.
- Develop stratagems and systems to ameliorate the unavoidable incursions of work into your personal life.
- Making the most of your non-working life is damned hard work.

## Keeping Your Balance

*Time Management*
- If you make work-lists, include personal, family decisions and actions as well as business decisions and actions.
- Get calendars of school events as far in advance as possible, and enter all the relevant dates in your diary pronto.
- Thinking about work at home while you are busy doing not a lot can deftly enhance your work/life balance without anyone noticing. (All competent managers can do at least two things at once – research suggests women are far better at it than men.)
- The more often you work through lunch-time the less often you will need to work at supper-time.
- Be picky about out-of-hours business invitations. Most business entertaining isn't that entertaining.

- Certain sectors, like retailing and catering, will inevitably eat into your time more than others. But even in these sectors some organisations care about work/life issues – and some don't.
- If you burn out you lose out. It's a lose-lose-lose situation – your career, your family and your health all fall sick.

## Families

- Create a 'family system'. If your partner is at work too, correlate your diaries at the start of each week.
- When you have been endlessly travelling or working endless hours for endless weeks, redress the balance with a family treat – an unscheduled family holiday, or at least a long weekend.
- Spend as much time as you can, while you can, with your parents.
- At weekends, whenever possible turn business activities into family outings.
- On long business trips, go shopping. Not for you, for them.

## Partners

- Career changes affect partners too: consultation beforehand will save recrimination later.
- Tell your partner about all serious financial commitments. It isn't legally required, but it should be.
- Get away with your partner – without your children – from time to time.
- Partners who play together stay together. If your leisure interests are incompatible you'll end up spending your spare time as well as your work time in separate worlds.
- If you both go out to work, share family organisational responsibilities equally - and always ensure you both think the share is fair.

- Let both your partner and your PA know how you can be contacted in an emergency.
- If you need time to unwind in the evening, or to wind yourself up in the morning, tell your partner. Misunderstood silences are not so much golden as red rags to a bull.
- Involve your partner in your organisation's social events.
- Telephone your partner as often as you can when you are travelling (and chat to your children if they're around).
- Go out on a date with your partner at least once a week.
- Do not be too proud, too macho, or too scared to tell your partner about your business failures as well as your successes.

## Children

- Finding really good people to look after your children is tough. Do not skimp on the time and effort required.
- Take your children to your workplace now and again, explain what you do, introduce them to everyone – before long their advice will be more valuable than that of most management consultants, and a helluva lot cheaper.
- Whenever your children call with an urgent message speak to them immediately – and let them know they should not insist on interrupting you except when really necessary.
- Get involved with your children's schools. This will both show an interest in their education and be an education for you.
- Getting away alone for a few days with your children is a great way of getting to know them.

## Friends

- Make friends with people from many walks of life, outside of your industry. Their perspectives will enhance your perspectives.

- If you live far from your job and frequently have to stay away overnight, instead of working late each evening make a point of arranging to see your friends – many of whom, like you, probably find themselves alone and footloose during the week.
- Before turning business acquaintances into personal friends, try to ensure both your partners will be friends too. Otherwise your new friendship will become an additional strain on your work/life balance, instead of an additional bond.
- Friends can often see our problems more clearly than we can ourselves. Occasionally ask them how you are handling your work/life balance. If they say you are not handling things terribly well, it means you are handling things terribly badly.

### Travelling and Commuting

- If you work in London but live too far away to commute each night, bust a gut to get a place in town where your wife and children can occasionally come and stay.
- Be wary of living above the shop. When your life and your work snuggle up that closely they cannot easily be divorced, which could well mean you will be.
- When you are travelling far, switch to the new local time immediately you arrive and don't look back (except before you phone home!).
- Before joining a multinational organisation explore the likelihood of being sent abroad. If it is high, make sure they will make everything work smoothly for you and your family – both on the way out, and on the way back.
- Before phoning from abroad check the time at home.

### At Work

- Learn by watching other people and emulate those you admire.

Workaholics and slackers should – like bushtailed phascogales – be studied, not copied.

- Make clear to everyone who reports to you that you respect their need to achieve a proper work/life balance, and you will always be sympathetic to their personal needs.

- Do as you would be done by: do not telephone business colleagues at unreasonable times, and always ask whether they would prefer to call you back later.

- While on maternity or paternity leave, keep in touch with what is happening at work by e-mail.

- Never blur the issue when you take time off for family reasons. Be totally truthful – both for yourself and for the wider cause of everyone's work/life balance.

- Get important business papers distributed in time for people to read them at weekends. All managers expect to do some reading at the weekend, and it will help them cope better during the week.

- Create your own 'personal' days by holding back a week or more of your holiday entitlement and taking it a day or two at a time.

- When applying for jobs make sure your prospective employers really mean what they say about work/life balance. While they are checking on your references, you check on theirs.

- Likewise, you should make clear to prospective employers how much time you intend to devote to your children. If you don't hoist a warning signal up-front you'll crash into buffers later.

## At Leisure

- Choose leisure interests you can combine with work: photography, golf – even ornithology – are all ideal for globetrotters.

- Put something back into society. Working to improve the lives of others is a surefire way to improve the balance of your own work and life.
- When posted abroad join local clubs and societies and – better still – get your partner to be a joiner too.
- If you have profound strong convictions do not let work impede them.

## Getting it Right

- Once you have decided on your priorities, go for them. If that means shifting important meetings or failing to have a drink in the pub of an evening because you prefer to be with your family – too bad.
- Analyse your own work/life balance now and again. Try not to view it either too harshly or through rose-tinted spectacles. If it seems wrong, change things. Whether you like it or not, you will end up reviewing the balance in years to come, and by then it will be too late to make amends.

## In Times of Trouble

- Working long and hard can – and does – help people cope with terrible moments in their lives. Sometimes work keeps life in balance.

This list lays no claim to be exhaustive. You can almost certainly add a few ideas of your own. The most important balancing act I myself instigated was to ensure we always had babysitters on call, so that when I arrived home tired and tetchy my wife and I could nip out for a consoling meal or a movie. Having babysitters on call is no big deal; it simply needs organising. Most of the stratagems and systems above are not big deals. Make a few of them happen, and your work/life balance will be immeasurably improved.

Finally we return, with Professor Drucker, to the question of time. The first and most essential element in achieving a satisfactory work/life balance is the achievement of a satisfactory Work/Life Ratio. If your Ratio is seriously out of kilter you are riding for a fall. If you spend far less than half your Basic Waking Week with your family, then you will not see enough of them over the long haul to relate closely to them. Out of sight, out of mind. Absence can make the heart grow colder.

Some people – the people Richard Sykes calls 'mad', and Dennis Stevenson calls 'obsessional little twits' – are happy to let their work/life balance plunge to hell in a handbasket. If that is your preference, so be it. Though it is impossible to define – let alone to achieve – a perfect work/life balance, we can all recognise a sickly one. The symptoms are self-evident. If your family life is a succession of squabbles and quarrels about lack of time, lack of commitment and lack of caring, followed by sullen and smouldering silences, then you can bet your next salary rise to a cancelled holiday that your work/life balance is chronically sick. Ignore the symptoms and your stress level will go up, your productivity at work will go down and your family life will deteriorate like a festering sore. Fortunately, if your work/life sickness is not yet terminal – and it probably isn't – it can still be cured.

You have just read how 16 people who have climbed to the very top of the business ladder still have great family lives. In nearly every case they started out on the lowest rung, and when they started out the general level of corporate sympathy for work/life problems was zilch – or even less than zilch: women had to lie about spending time with their children, men who worried too much about their personal lives were viewed as wimps. This book is packed with revealing hints and tips on how to balance your work and personal lives, but the real secret is that there is no secret. Nothing works better than working at it: aim to improve your work/life balance and your work/life balance will improve.

Go for it!

# Index